# JUMP START SINATRA

BY DARREN JONES

D0825784

# Jump Start Sinatra

by Darren Jones

Copyright © 2013 SitePoint Pty. Ltd.

**Product Manager**: Simon Mackie     **Expert Reviewer**: Konstantin Haase
**Technical Editor**: Diana MacDonald     **English Editor**: Kelly Steele
**Indexer**: Glenda Browne     **Cover Designer**: Alex Walker

Published by SitePoint Pty. Ltd.

48 Cambridge Street Collingwood
VIC Australia 3066
Web: www.sitepoint.com
Email: business@sitepoint.com

ISBN 978-0-9873321-4-1 (print)

ISBN 978-0-9873321-5-8 (ebook)
Printed and bound in the United States of America

## Dedication

To Mum and Dad ... thanks for being awesome!

## About the Author

Darren Jones has been playing around with programming and building websites for over a decade. In 2007, he discovered Ruby and Rails; they were both great, but then he found Sinatra and fell in love with its classy approach to web development. At the start of 2010, Darren started the "I Did It My Way" blog, detailing his quest to master Sinatra, and at the end of that year he used Sinatra to build the Cards in the Cloud website.[1]

Darren writes Sinatra tutorials for RubySource,[2] and lives in the city of Manchester, where he enjoys playing water polo and teaching mathematics.

## About the Expert Reviewer

As maintainer of Sinatra, Konstantin Haase is an Open Source developer by heart. Ruby has become his language of choice since 2005. He regularly contributes to widespread projects, including Rubinius, Rack, Rails, and MRI. In 2012, he received the Ruby Hero Award for his outstanding contributions to the community. He now works on Open Source projects at Travis CI in Berlin, Germany.

## About SitePoint

SitePoint specializes in publishing fun, practical, and easy-to-understand content for web professionals. Visit http://www.sitepoint.com/ to access our blogs, books, newsletters, articles, and community forums. You'll find a stack of information on JavaScript, PHP, Ruby, mobile development, design, and more.

## About Jump Start

Jump Start books provide you with a rapid and practical introduction to web development languages and technologies. Typically around 150 pages in length, they can be read in a weekend, giving you a solid grounding in the topic and the confidence to experiment on your own.

---

[1] http://cardsinthecloud.com/
[2] http://rubysource.com/

# Table of Contents

# Preface

Jump Start Sinatra is a short book, but I see it as being like Sinatra itself—packing a punch despite its size. The book you hold in your hands will take you on a roller-coaster tour of Sinatra, demonstrating various tasks by example. We jump straight into using Sinatra in Chapter One, before going on to build a fully modular, database-driven dynamic website that even has some Ajax thrown in for good measure!

I first started using Sinatra about three years ago, and very quickly fell for its classy approach to web development. I was a complete beginner, and despite there being few tutorials around, I quickly picked up the basics to enjoy the flexibility that using Sinatra gave me.

This book is everything I've learned about Sinatra collected together in one place. In my opinion, Sinatra is as close to perfect as a piece of software can be. It does everything it needs to and nothing more; there isn't a single line of bloat anywhere in its source code, which weighs in at fewer than 2,000 lines!

Sinatra applications often have a certain finesse, with code that's easy to read and follow. Sinatra puts you in the driver's seat, allowing you to make the application as simple or as complicated as it needs to be; all the decisions are down to you. Sinatra's direct simplicity makes it easy for you to implement those decisions with minimal fuss.

Opinions abound that Sinatra can only be used for small applications or simple APIs, but this simply isn't true. While it is a perfect fit for these tasks, Sinatra also scales impressively, demonstrated by the fact that it's been used to power some big production sites.

Sinatra is only small, but it is powerful and flexible. You're really only limited by what Ruby can do … and Ruby can do pretty much anything you can imagine! It is my hope that by the time you finish reading this book, you'll have learned enough to go forward with Sinatra and start building exciting web applications, big or small.

Whatever you do, I'd love to hear how you get along.

# Who Should Read This Book

*Jump Start Sinatra* is aimed at all levels of Ruby programmers, particularly those who have used Ruby on Rails. While learning Ruby falls outside the scope of this book, a beginner should be able to follow along with the examples. It should also be of interest to anyone who has used other web development languages or frameworks such as PHP or Django. The book assumes no familiarity with Sinatra, and so begins with installing it and creating a very basic application.

# Conventions Used

You'll notice that we've used certain typographic and layout styles throughout this book to signify different types of information. Look out for the following items.

## Code Samples

Code in this book will be displayed using a fixed-width font, like so:

```
<h1>A Perfect Summer's Day</h1>
<p>It was a lovely day for a walk in the park. The birds
were singing and the kids were all back at school.</p>
```

If the code is to be found in the book's code archive, the name of the file will appear at the top of the program listing, like this:

example.css

```
.footer {
  background-color: #CCC;
  border-top: 1px solid #333;
}
```

If only part of the file is displayed, this is indicated by the word *excerpt*:

example.css *(excerpt)*

```
  border-top: 1px solid #333;
```

If additional code is to be inserted into an existing example, the new code will be displayed in bold:

```
function animate() {
  new_variable = "Hello";
}
```

Also, where existing code is required for context, rather than repeat all the code, a ⋮ will be displayed:

```
function animate() {
  ⋮
  return new_variable;
}
```

Some lines of code are intended to be entered on one line, but we've had to wrap them because of page constraints. A ➥ indicates a line break that exists for formatting purposes only, and should be ignored.

```
URL.open("http://rubysource.com/rails-or-sinatra-the-best-of-both-w
➥orlds/");
```

## Tips, Notes, and Warnings

 **Hey, You!**

Tips will give you helpful little pointers.

 **Ahem, Excuse Me ...**

Notes are useful asides that are related—but not critical—to the topic at hand. Think of them as extra tidbits of information.

 **Make Sure You Always ...**

... pay attention to these important points.

 **Watch Out!**

Warnings will highlight any gotchas that are likely to trip you up along the way.

## Supplementary Materials

**http://www.sitepoint.com/books/sinatra1/**
The book's website, containing links, updates, resources, and more.

**http://www.sitepoint.com/books/sinatra1/code.php**
The downloadable code archive for this book.

**http://www.sitepoint.com/forums/forumdisplay.php?227-Ruby-amp-Rails**
SitePoint's Ruby and Rails forum, for help on any tricky Ruby problems. If you have Sinatra problems, try http://www.sinatrarb.com/.

**books@sitepoint.com**
Our email address, should you need to contact us for support, to report a problem, or for any other reason.

## Challenge Yourself

Once you've mastered Sinatra, test yourself with our online quiz. With questions based on the book's content, only true Sinatra virtuosos can achieve a perfect score. Head on over to http://quizpoint.com/#categories/SINATRA.

## Friends of SitePoint

Thanks for buying this book. We really appreciate your support! We now think of you as a "Friend of SitePoint," and so would like to invite you to our special page: http://sitepoint.com/friends. Here you can SAVE up to 43% on a range of other super-cool SitePoint products, just by using the password: **friends**.

## Acknowledgments

Thanks to Aaron Osteraas for getting the process started. Thanks to Simon for making it happen. Thanks to Di and Kelly for spotting all the gaffes I made. Thanks to Glenn for all his support at RubySource. Big thanks to Konstantin for making Sinatra what it is today and for all his great help and advice. Thanks to Baily for getting me into this web development thing. And a special thank you to Helen for always being there for me.

# Sinatra Takes to the Stage

Congratulations for picking up and reading this little book about Sinatra. Since its release in 2007, Sinatra has quickly gained in popularity in the Ruby web community due to its elegant simplicity and classy syntax. Everybody who uses it falls in love with its elegant simplicity and classy syntax. This book will introduce you to Sinatra from installation right through to building your own web application and hosting it on the Internet. So, without further ado, let's get on with the show!

## What is Sinatra?

You might be wondering what Sinatra is. Here's what the Sinatra website has to say: "Sinatra is a DSL for quickly creating web applications in Ruby with minimal effort."[1]

What does that mean? Well, a DSL (domain-specific language) is a language that's designed to be implemented in a particular domain; that's in contrast to general-purpose languages that are created to solve problems in several domains. Sinatra is a lightweight Ruby library that makes access to HTTP much easier. Ruby is a

---

[1] http://www.sinatrarb.com/intro

simple but powerful object-oriented programming language; its elegant syntax makes it both expressive and powerful. HTTP is the protocol that powers the Web.

## Hypertext Transfer Protocol

HTTP is the Hypertext Transfer Protocol, and it's what makes the Web go round. This network protocol allows communication over the Internet between clients and servers. A client (such as a web browser) will request a resource (usually a web page) from a server, which processes the request and sends back a response to the client. This response contains a status code (usually 200, which indicates that everything is okay), and the requested resource that's usually in the form of a web page. The requests and responses are messages sent via HTTP. Figure 1.1 shows how that works.

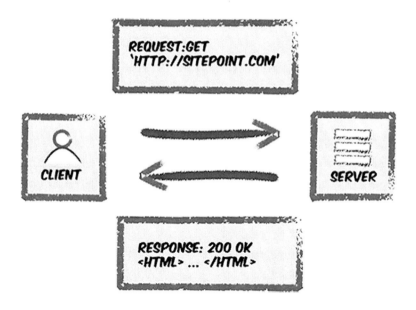

Figure 1.1. Traditional client–server model

Sinatra makes it easy—trivial almost—to build sites, services, and web apps using Ruby. A Sinatra application is basically made up of one or more Ruby files. You don't need to be an expert Rubyist to use Sinatra, but the more Ruby you know, the better you'll be at building Sinatra apps. And besides, Ruby is such a brilliantly expressive language that it would be a shame not to learn it! On the flip side, learning Sinatra and studying other people's code will definitely help to improve your Ruby skills. I mentioned earlier that Sinatra is a lightweight library, with under 2,000 lines of Ruby code. This is well worth knowing, as it will help you understand how Sinatra works—and you'll also see lots of examples of great Ruby code!

Sinatra was written in 2007 by Blake Mizerany, and has steadily gained in popularity. At the time of writing, there have been over 3.5 million downloads of Sinatra on the RubyGems website[2] since it was hosted there in 2010. It has simplicity at its heart, but is capable of creating large database-driven websites and is used by sites such as the BBC, GitHub, LinkedIn, and even Apple to power its Podcast Library.[3] It has also spawned numerous clones for different languages, including Express (Node) https://github.com/visionmedia/express, Slim (PHP) https://github.com/codeguy/Slim, Flask (Python) http://flask.pocoo.org/, Spark (Java) http://www.sparkjava.com/, and Nancy (.NET) http://nancyfx.org/.

Unlike Ruby on Rails, Sinatra is definitely not a framework. It's without conventions and imposes no file structure on you whatsoever. Sinatra apps are basically just Ruby programs; what Sinatra does is connect them to the Web. Rather than hide behind lots of magic, it exposes the way the Web works by making the key concepts of HTTP verbs and URLs an explicit part of it. This means that you can build big and powerful database-driven sites with Sinatra, doing it your way without being constrained by any enforced conventions. Having said that, we know that with great power comes great responsibility, so having free rein to do anything you like can also be a pitfall. Sinatra won't stop you from writing bad code!

Sinatra is built on top of Rack,[4] which is a low-level interface that communicates between an HTTP server and a Ruby object. Most Ruby web frameworks such as Rails, Ramaze, Rango, Camping, and Halcyon also sit on top of Rack. This makes Sinatra easy to extend using its own extension API, RubyGems (libraries written in Ruby—Sinatra is one!), and Rack Middleware. This opens up a world of possibilities for extending your application and avoids you having to reinvent the wheel.

Oh … and in case you were wondering, it is named after Frank Sinatra, apparently because he had "so much class he deserves a web-framework named after him."[5]

---

[2] http://rubygems.org/
[3] http://www.sinatrarb.com/wild.html
[4] http://rack.github.com/
[5] http://www.sinatrarb.com/about

## Why should you use Sinatra?

Sinatra lets you write simple yet elegant code that produces amazing results. Its simplicity means that you can create a fully functional web app in just one file. There are no complicated setup procedures or configuration to worry about. You can just open up a text editor and get started with minimal effort, leaving you to focus on the needs of your application. There's also little waste, with code restricted to just what is needed to kick off.

Developing in Sinatra is perfect for prototyping ideas and sites. Its syntax is basic enough to pick up, yet very powerful. Sinatra is extremely flexible—it gets out of your way and lets you do things how you want. If you can build it in Ruby, you can make it into a Sinatra app. For anything from the smallest of microsites to a full-scale web application, it's the perfect choice for API implementations, Middleware, widgets, Facebook apps, and more.

And last but by no means least, you'll find an amazingly supportive community around Sinatra. The online documentation[6] is first rate and there are always helpful people on the Google Groups page[7] willing to pass on their knowledge. There's also the #sinatra channel on the Freenode IRC network, and numerous articles that appear on the RubySource website[8] (some of them written by yours truly!) that can help develop your Sinatra skills.

# Installing Sinatra

Before installing Sinatra, make sure you have Ruby and RubyGems installed on your system. This is fairly straightforward, but differs depending on which operating system you use. Below are instructions for Windows, Linux, and Mac OS X.

## Windows

The easiest way to install Ruby and RubyGems if you use Windows is to use the Ruby Installer.[9] Once you have installed Ruby using the installer, it's simply a case of installing Sinatra with the following line:

---

[6] http://www.sinatrarb.com/intro.html

[7] https://groups.google.com/forum/?fromgroups#!forum/sinatrarb

[8] http://rubysource.com/

[9] http://rubyinstaller.org/

```
$ gem install sinatra
```

## GNU/Linux

You can use your favorite package manager to install Ruby in most flavors of GNU/Linux. For example, in recent versions of Ubuntu (and other Debian-based distros), you can use the following command:

```
$ sudo apt-get install ruby1.9.1
```

After you have installed Ruby, you'll need to download and install the most recent version of the RubyGems package manager.[10]

Alternatively, if you want a more up-to-date version, you can use the Ruby Version Manager.[11] This will also install RubyGems.

Now you can install Sinatra with the following line:

```
$ sudo gem install sinatra
```

## Mac

Most Mac systems will already have Ruby installed, although it's usually the older 1.8 version of Ruby. I'd recommend updating to a more recent version of Ruby (currently 1.9 at the time of writing). This can be done using Homebrew[12] and the following command:

```
$ brew install ruby
```

This also installs RubyGems. Now you can install Sinatra with the following line:

```
$ gem install sinatra
```

---

[10] http://rubygems.org/pages/download
[11] https://rvm.io/rvm/install/
[12] http://mxcl.github.com/homebrew/

# Your First Sinatra App

I'm sure that by now you're itching to write some code, so let's get to it. We're going to start out with the most basic of Sinatra apps (four lines, no less!), and then show off some of the fundamentals before writing a mini-casino app by the end of the chapter.

Open a text editor (such as Notepad, gedit, or TextEdit) and write the following code. Save it as **hello.rb**:

*chapter01/hello.rb (excerpt)*

```ruby
require 'sinatra'

get '/hello' do
  "Hello Sinatra!"
end
```

And that's all you need for a Sinatra app. The first line is a Ruby `require` statement that pulls in all the code from the Sinatra library; it's needed in all Sinatra apps. The next block of code is what's known as a **route handler**. It starts with the HTTP verb `get`, and says that the client should get the page with the URL of /hello. The last line of the handler is always evaluated and sent to the browser; in this case it was the string `Hello Sinatra!`.

Sinatra apps run on a server, so we'll need to spin one up. Open up a terminal and navigate to the folder where the **hello.rb** file is saved. Enter the following command:

```
$ ruby hello.rb
```

 **Up to Old Tricks**

If you are running Ruby version 1.8, you'll have to run it using `ruby --rubygems hello.rb`.

You should see a similar output to this:

```
== Sinatra/1.3.3 has taken the stage on 4567 for development with
backup from WEBrick
>> INFO WEBrick::HTTPServer#start: pid=2206 port=4567
```

To stop the server running, hold down **Ctrl** and press **C**.

### Getting Comfy with the Terminal

When developing with Sinatra, you'll often find yourself using the terminal or command prompt. This can be scary at first, but it really isn't anything to worry about and will soon seem like second nature.

Now open up your browser and navigate to http://localhost:4567/hello (localhost is your own computer and 4567 is the port that Sinatra runs on by default). You should see a similar sight to the screenshot in Figure 1.2.

Figure 1.2. Your first Sinatra app!

That's it, your first Sinatra app. It really is that simple. Let's add another route handler to the bottom of **hello.rb**:

chapter01/hello.rb (excerpt)

```ruby
get '/frank' do
  name = "Frank"
  "Hello #{name}"
end
```

This handler contains a bit of Ruby code. We set a variable called name to be Frank and then insert into the string saying "Hello." As much Ruby as you like can go before the last line (before the word end), but it's only that last line that's evaluated and sent to the browser. The last line is an example of an **interpolated variable** inside a string, where anything inside #{ … } will be evaluated and placed inside the string; in this case, the variable name evaluates to "Frank," so this is placed within the string.

As we've made a change to the code, we have to restart the server. Go back to the terminal and hold down **Ctrl-C**. Type in `ruby hello.rb` again and navigate to http://localhost:4567/frank in your browser, where you should now see "Hello Frank."

 **Sinatra::Reloader**

Restarting the server after every change to your existing files can become tiresome, so it's worth using Sinatra::Reloader, which is part of the Sinatra::Contrib library (more on this later). To use Sinatra::Reloader, install the `sinatra-contrib` gem:

```
$ gem install sinatra-contrib
```

Then add the following line to your files (underneath the `require 'sinatra'` line):

chapter01/hello.rb *(excerpt)*

```
require 'sinatra'
require 'sinatra/reloader' if development?
```

Now all you need to do is reload the page for any changes to your existing code to take place!

# Variables and Named Parameters

This is all well and good, but what if we don't know the user's name in advance—can we make a more generalized URL that will say hello to anybody? Of course we can! Add the following route handler to the bottom of **hello.rb**:

chapter01/hello.rb *(excerpt)*

```
get '/:name' do
  name = params[:name]
  "Hi there #{name}!"
end
```

This route contains what is known as a named parameter, called `:name`, signified by the leading colon. **Named parameters** can go anywhere in a URL, and are available in the handler as part of the `params` hash. A hash is like a storage box that uses a key/value pair system of storing data; for example, you could have this hash:

```
ages = {bart: 10, lisa: 8, maggie: 1}
```

Here, `bart` is a key and `10` is its value. You would reference an item in the hash using the key; for example, if you wanted to know Lisa's age, you'd use `ages[:lisa]`.

The `params` hash is automatically created to hold any information that is entered as named parameters in the URL, or as a parameter submitted via an HTML form (more on that in the section called "Creating New Songs" in Chapter 3!). In our example, the key is `:name` and the value will be whatever is entered in the URL. This is a great way of grabbing information from a URL. You should see the message displayed in Figure 1.3 if you go to http://localhost:4567/daz in your browser.

Figure 1.3. Introducing daz

Sinatra processes the route handlers from top to bottom; as soon as it finds a match to the URL entered, it will process that handler. You can see this by going to http://localhost:4567/frank. Technically, this is covered in our general route and you might expect to see the message "Hi there frank!"; however, as there is another route that matches this URL earlier in the code, that's what is processed, so the message shown is "`Hello Frank`."

For more of an idea of how the `params` hash works, add the following route handler to the bottom of **hello.rb**:

```
chapter01/hello.rb (excerpt)
get '/:one/:two/:three' do
  "first: #{params[:one]}, second: #{params[:two]}, third: #{params[
➥:three]}"
end
```

Now if you navigate to http://localhost:4567/bolt/blake/gatlin, you should see as per Figure 1.4.

Figure 1.4. A result of Olympic proportions

Here's another example that shows how we can fetch data entered in the URL and process it using some of Ruby's methods; in this case, we're using the Time class:

```
chapter01/hello.rb (excerpt)
get '/what/time/is/it/in/:number/hours' do
  number = params[:number].to_i
  time = Time.now + number * 3600
  "The time in #{number} hours will be #{time.strftime('%I:%M %p')}"
end
```

Now, if you go to http://localhost:4567/what/time/is/it/in/3/hours (Figure 1.5), you'll gain a glimpse of the future.

Figure 1.5. In the future, the time will be ...

**Exercise for the Ruby Newbs**

There was a lot of Ruby in that last example, mainly used to manipulate the date and time. I'll avoid going into explaining it all here, but recommend you have a look online at what some of the code is doing. This is what my old school textbooks used to call "an exercise for the interested reader."

# Creating a Betting Game

Let's finish off the chapter with a fun and quick example of what you can do with Sinatra. We're going to create a little dice-betting game. You place a bet on a number from one to six (you can actually enter any values, but you're not going to win that way, are you?) via the URL, and then see if your number comes up.

Create a new file called **bet.rb** and enter the following code:

```
                                                          chapter01/bet.rb

require 'sinatra'

get '/bet/:stake/on/:number' do
  stake = params[:stake].to_i
  number = params[:number].to_i
  roll = rand(6) + 1
  if number == roll
    "It landed on #{roll}. Well done, you win #{6*stake} chips"
  else
    "It landed on #{roll}. You lose your stake of #{stake} chips"
  end
end
```

Save the file and then start the server by entering this command in a terminal:

```
$ ruby bet.rb
```

Now open your browser and try to predict what number has come up; for example, if 5 is your lucky number and you have lots of fake money to fritter away, you could try betting using the URL http://localhost:4567/bet/1000000/on/5. The result is shown in Figure 1.6.

Figure 1.6. Not your lucky day

This example shows that you can put quite a bit of Ruby logic into the route handler before you send anything back to the server. In this case, we grab the amount the user bets and the number they bet on from the URL, and then save them as variables. We then generate a random number between one and six using Ruby's rand method to mimic the rolling of dice. To finish, we use a bit of conditional logic to determine which message to send back to the browser depending on the outcome.

### What's all this to_i business?

You might be wondering why we had to put to_i on the end of the params hashes in the last couple of examples. Ruby is an object-orientated language, which means everything is an object with methods. Methods are accessed using dot notation. to_i is a method that converts strings into integers so that we can perform mathematical tasks with them (to_i stands for "to integer"). Any values that are obtained from URLs in the params hash are always given as strings, so if you want the numerical form, remember to use the to_i method!

# Sinatra: The Safe Bet

In this chapter, we looked at what Sinatra is and isn't, and why you should be using it for developing web applications. We installed Ruby, RubyGems, and Sinatra, and then got our hands dirty with some code, creating some simple route handlers to show off how Sinatra works. We finished by creating a little betting game web app.

We're now ready to roll out some web pages using HTML in the next chapter, so what are you waiting for?

# Building a Basic Website

In the last chapter, we installed Sinatra and played around with routes and handlers; however, we only ever sent plain strings back to the client, which, let's face it, has its limits. In most cases, we'll want to send HTML pages for the browser to show. As usual, Sinatra makes this really easy to achieve.

In this chapter, we'll look at using views to send HTML to the browser, and start to build a basic website comprising navigable pages. We'll use templating languages such as ERB (embedded Ruby) and Slim to produce the HTML, and utilize the CSS preprocessor, Sass, to create a stylesheet to make the site look prettier.

## Example Website: Songs By Sinatra

The website we'll be building is called "Songs By Sinatra," and will showcase Frank Sinatra songs. We'll build some basic pages in this chapter and then develop it over the course of the book. We will start with the typical pages that many websites use:

- Home
- About
- Contact

Initially, we'll create some static HTML pages with navigation to each page. Create a new file called **main.rb** and enter the following code:

chapter02/main.rb *(excerpt)*

```
require 'sinatra'

get '/' do
  erb :home
end
```

This is just like the route handlers we saw in the section called "Your First Sinatra App" in Chapter 1, except that instead of finishing with a string that's sent back to the browser, we finish with the statement `erb :home`. It's a reference to what is known as a **view**, which is a representation of data, such as markup that is sent to the browser. It is usually written in a templating language that's translated into HTML before being sent back to the browser. We'll start by using ERB to create our views. This can be seen in the route handler; the `erb` method is used with the argument `:home` to indicate that `erb` should be used to render the view called "home."

The name of the view needs to be a symbol. The server then finds the relevant view and sends the HTML back to the browser.

 **Symbols**

Symbols in Ruby are similar to string objects. They always start with a colon, and may or may not be inside quotes. If it contains spaces, it must be in quotes. Here are some examples:

```
:name
:first_name
:'last name'
```

So how do these differ from strings? Well, it's subtle, but two identical symbols are represented by the same object, whereas two identical strings are represented by two distinct objects. For example, if you use the `:name` symbol in different parts of your code, the symbol is referring to the same object as far as Ruby is concerned. If, however, you use the string `"name"`, Ruby will create a new object every time you reference the string `"name"` in the code. This might seem like a minor detail, but using symbols saves a lot of memory by only using one object. It's particularly useful when they're employed repeatedly; in keys used in a hash, for example. In fact, we've already seen symbols used in the `params` hash: `params[:name]`.

# ERB and Views

ERB is short for Embedded Ruby and is a templating language that comes bundled with Ruby. It can be used to create HTML views that also contain Ruby code.

ERB is a superset of HTML, so plain old vanilla HTML is perfectly legal ERB code. To start with, create a simple HTML view. Where do we put this? Right in the same file! Just add the following to the bottom of **main.rb**:

*chapter02/main.rb (excerpt)*

```
__END__
@@home
<!doctype html>
<html lang="en">
<head>
  <title>Songs By Sinatra</title>
  <meta charset="utf-8">
</head>
<body>
  <header>
    <h1>Songs By Sinatra</h1>
    <nav>
      <ul>
        <li><a href="/" title="Home">Home</a></li>
        <li><a href="/about" title="About">About</a></li>
        <li><a href="/contact" title="Contact">Contact</a></li>
      </ul>
    </nav>
  </header>
  <section>
    <p>Welcome to this website all about the songs of the great
      Frank Sinatra</p>
  </section>
</body>
</html>
```

This is an example of one of Sinatra's coolest features: **inline views**. You can place any views that you want to use in your app at the bottom of the file after the `__END__` declaration. Each view starts with `@@`, followed by its name (`home` in this case).

If you start the server by typing `ruby main.rb` into a terminal and then go to http://localhost:4567/ in your browser, you should see a similar sight to Figure 2.1.

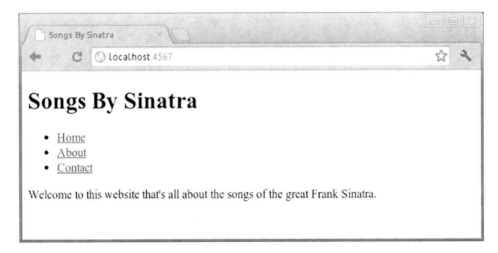

Figure 2.1. Your first inline view: bare-bones Sinatra

It's very basic and the links are currently broken, but at least we have a page of HTML!

# Becoming Dynamic

Since we're using ERB to create our views, we don't have to restrict ourselves to just using HTML. ERB lets you embed Ruby statements in the HTML, as it is basically a superset of HTML that adds two new tags:

```
<% ... %>
```

These tags contain any Ruby code that is meant to be invisible to the user (such as variable assignments and logic statements):

```
<%= ... %>
```

These tags are used for output; any Ruby code inside these tags will be evaluated and the output is then displayed in the browser.

To demonstrate how these tags work, let's add a variable called `title` to our view. To set a variable, we need to use `<% title = "Songs By Sinatra" %>`. We can then reference this variable anywhere else in the view. To display the title, we can use <%= title %>. This will evaluate the value of the variable and display the string Songs By Sinatra. To see this approach in action, change the home view so that it looks like the following:

```
                                                chapter02/main.rb (excerpt)

@@home
<% title="Songs By Sinatra" %>
<!doctype html>
<html lang="en">
<head>
  <title><%= title %></title>
  <meta charset="utf-8">
</head>
<body>
  <header>
    <h1><%= title %></h1>
```

If you restart the server (or just refresh the page if you're using Sinatra::Reloader), you won't see any difference; this is just what we expected, only now we're using variables for outputting the title.

## DRYing Out with Layouts

We can add as many views as we like using inline views, but we'd end up repeating a lot of the view code since most pages will have the same HTML at the start and end (the head section, for example). As well as being tedious, such repetition is considered bad practice. The principle of Don't Repeat Yourself (DRY for short) is almost gospel in the Ruby world. In essence, it means that you should avoid repeating lots of the same view code. And how do we do that? With layouts!

A layout is a special view because it's included in every other view, so it will be displayed on every page. This makes them perfect for storing any code that will be shown on every page like HTML headers and footers, CSS files, and any global JavaScript.

By default, Sinatra will automatically use any file called layout as the layout. Here's an example of how we could move a lot of the previous example into a layout view:

chapter02/main.rb *(excerpt)*

```ruby
require 'sinatra'

get '/' do
  erb :home
end


__END__
@@layout
<% title="Songs By Sinatra" %>
<!doctype html>
<html lang="en">
<head>
  <title><%= title %></title>
  <meta charset="utf-8">
</head>
<body>
  <header>
    <h1><%= title %></h1>
    <nav>
      <ul>
        <li><a href="/" title="Home">Home</a></li>
        <li><a href="/about" title="About">About</a></li>
        <li><a href="/contact" title="Contact">Contact</a></li>
      </ul>
    </nav>
  </header>
  <section>
    <%= yield %>
  </section>
</body>
</html>
@@home
<p>Welcome to this website that's all about the songs of the great
  Frank Sinatra.</p>
```

All that we've done here is move some of the code that will appear on all the pages into the view called `layout`. The important part of this view is the `yield` method in the middle. This is the point where the actual view called is displayed. So in this example, when we ask for the `home` view, the layout will be displayed with the content of the `home` view presented inside the `section` tags. Again, restarting the server (or refreshing the page in Sinatra::Reloader) will reveal no difference visually, as expected.

To show how the layout can save us time by avoiding repetition, we're now going to create the About and Contact pages. Now that we have our layout, we only have to create the HTML code that's relevant to each page.

Below is the code that adds the routes and views for the About page and Contact page. To keep it short, we'll just write a short paragraph for each page at this stage. Here's the full code for **main.rb** with the new routes and views added:

*chapter02/main.rb (excerpt)*

```ruby
require 'sinatra'

get '/' do
  erb :home
end

get '/about' do
  erb :about
end

get '/contact' do
  erb :contact
end

__END__
@@layout
<% title="Songs By Sinatra" %>
<!doctype html>
<html lang="en">
<head>
  <title><%= title %></title>
  <meta charset="utf-8">
</head>
<body>
  <header>
    <h1><%= title %></h1>
    <nav>
      <ul>
        <li><a href="/" title="Home">Home</a></li>
        <li><a href="/about" title="About">About</a></li>
        <li><a href="/contact" title="Contact">Contact</a></li>
      </ul>
    </nav>
  </header>
```

```
  <section>
    <%= yield %>
  </section>
</body>
</html>
@@home
<p>Welcome to this website that's all about the songs of the great
  Frank Sinatra.</p>

@@about
<p>This site is a demonstration of how to build a website using
  Sinatra.</p>

@@contact
<p>You can contact me by sending an email to daz at gmail.com</p>
```

As you can see, without the layout code we'd have to repeat a large part of the HTML in each view!

We now have a basic site up and running—not bad for one file and roughly 40 lines of code! If you restart the server, you should now be able to see the site in action and navigate from page to page.

Before we move on from layouts, I should point out that you can have several layouts that can be called whatever you like. If you want to use a different layout for a particular view, just add it as an option when you call the erb method. For example, if we wanted to use a special layout for the /contact route, we'd add the following option to the route handler:

```
get '/contact' do
  erb :contact, :layout => :special
end
```

Then we'd add a @@special layout to be used on the contact page.

## External Views

Now that we're starting to have a few views, it's become a bit crowded in our **main.rb** file. Inline views are great if you want to get a project built really quickly and the views are brief. But as soon as your site uses a number of more complex views, it can grow unwieldy, so it makes sense to separate the views into their own files.

This is very easy to do. All you need to do is save each view in a folder called **views**. Then save all your views as individual files inside this folder. This now means that inline views are unnecessary and we can remove them from **main.rb**. As you can see, it looks a lot leaner:

chapter02/main.rb *(excerpt)*

```ruby
require 'sinatra'

get '/' do
  erb :home
end

get '/about' do
  erb :about
end

get '/contact' do
  erb :contact
end
```

Now we have to save each view in its own file with the extension of **.erb**:

chapter02/views/layout.erb *(excerpt)*

```erb
<% title="Songs By Sinatra" %>
<!doctype html>
<html lang="en">
<head>
  <title><%= title %></title>
  <meta charset="utf-8">
</head>
<body>
  <header>
    <h1><%= title %></h1>
    <nav>
      <ul>
        <li><a href="/" title="Home">Home</a></li>
        <li><a href="/about" title="About">About</a></li>
        <li><a href="/contact" title="Contact">Contact</a></li>
      </ul>
    </nav>
  </header>
  <section>
```

```
      <%= yield %>
    </section>
  </body>
  </html>
```

chapter02/views/home.erb *(excerpt)*

```
<p>Welcome to this website that's all about the songs of the
  great Frank Sinatra.</p>
```

chapter02/views/about.erb

```
<p>This site is a demonstration of how to build a website using
  Sinatra.</p>
```

chapter02/views/contact.erb

```
<p>You can contact me by sending an email to daz at gmail.com</p>
```

## Folder Structure

Now that we've created a views folder, we can also add a public folder. This is where all public-facing assets are kept, such as images, CSS files, JavaScript files, and even static HTML pages. By default, this folder is named **public**, but this can be changed to anything you like by placing the following code in your **main.rb** file:

```
set :public_folder, 'assets'
```

Similarly, you can also change the name and path to the folder where Sinatra looks for the views:

```
set :views, 'templates'
```

Both of these examples use the set method, which is used by Sinatra to configure different settings. We'll be covering this in more detail in the section called "Settings" in Chapter 4.

This gives us a basic folder structure, as seen in Figure 2.2.

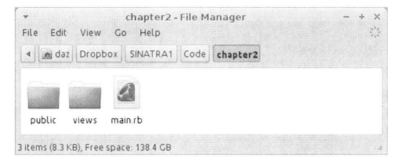

Figure 2.2. Our basic folder structure

## Enhancing with Images

Now that we have a public folder, we can use it to add images to our website. I created a logo using the cover art for this book and found a copyright-free picture of Frank Sinatra on Wikimedia Commons.[1] These can be placed inside a folder called **images** within the public folder and then used on the site. I also created a favicon based on the logo. This is the little icon that shows in the browser address bar when visiting the site. It should be saved in the root of the public directory and is usually requested automatically by the browser. If you'd like to use the same images, here are the links:

- Frank Sinatra picture: http://songs-by-sinatra.herokuapp.com/images/sinatra.jpg
- Website logo: http://songs-by-sinatra.herokuapp.com/images/logo.png
- Favicon: http://songs-by-sinatra.herokuapp.com/favicon.ico

To use the picture of Frank Sinatra on our Home page, we change **home.erb** to this:

chapter02/views/home.erb

```
<p>Welcome to this website that's all about the songs of the great
    Frank Sinatra.</p>
<img src="/images/sinatra.jpg" alt="Frank Sinatra">
```

Now, if you restart the server and reload the Home page, you should see a picture of Ol' Blue Eyes, as in Figure 2.3.

---

[1] http://commons.wikimedia.org

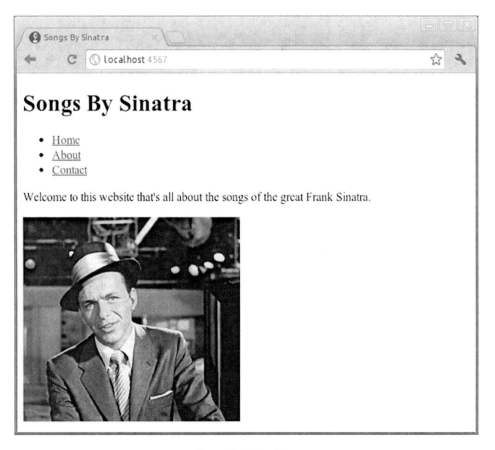

Figure 2.3. Ol' Blue Eyes

# Adding Some Style

Now that we have a public folder, let's add some CSS to make the site a bit prettier. To do this, we first need to create a global stylesheet that will apply styles to all the pages. Save this page in the **public** folder.

Here's some basic styling of headings and paragraphs, which includes our logo as a background image to the heading. Feel free to add more of your own styles (I named it simply **styles.css**):[2]

---

[2] If your CSS is limited and you'd like to expand on it, you could check out the amazing *CSS3 Anthology* by Rachel Andrew: http://www.sitepoint.com/books/cssant4/.

chapter02/views/styles.css

```css
h1 {
  color: #903;
  font: 32px/1 Helvetica, Arial, sans-serif;
}

header h1 {
  font-size: 40px;
  line-height: 80px;
  background: transparent url(/images/logo.png) 0 0 no-repeat;
  padding-left: 84px;
}

p {
  font: 13px/1.4 Helvetica, Arial, sans-serif;
}
```

Now we'll add a link to this file. It needs to be added to all the pages, so the best place to put it is in the layout. Open up **layout.erb** and edit the file to include a link to **styles.css**:

chapter02/views/layout.erb *(excerpt)*

```erb
<% title="Songs By Sinatra" %>
<!doctype html>
<html lang="en">
<head>
  <title><%= title %></title>
  <meta charset="utf-8">
  <link rel="stylesheet" href="styles.css">
</head>
```

Upon reloading the page, it should look more appealing, perhaps like Figure 2.4.

Figure 2.4. Sinatra with style

## Missing Pages

We now have three routes that users can navigate to on our site where they'll see the associated view. But what if they type a URL directly into the browser that's without a route handler?

If you try this now by going to http://localhost:4567/missing in your browser, you'll see Sinatra's standard "page missing" page. I have to say it's just as classy as the framework itself, as presented in Figure 2.5.

Figure 2.5. Sinatra's standard "page missing" page

The page also provides a helpful hint on how to create a route handler for that missing route—neat, huh? It's really just for development, though; the page looks different when in production mode. Still, it's good practice to have our own bespoke 404 error page for the site. Once again, this couldn't be simpler—Sinatra has a special method for that, called not_found. It's used just like the route handler blocks:

chapter02/main.rb *(excerpt)*

```
not_found do
  erb :not_found
end
```

This block refers to a view called `not_found` (I chose this name because it made sense, but you can call it whatever you like). We now need to create a file called **not_found.erb** and save it in the **views** folder. Let's keep the content simple for now:

*chapter02/views/not_found.erb*

```
<h2>4 Oh 4!</h2>
<p> The page you are looking for is missing. Why not go back to the
  <a href='/'>home page</a> and start over?</p>
```

 **HTTP Status Codes**

404 is perhaps the most well known of all the HTTP status codes, but there are plenty of others. In fact, the server sends a status code with every response to a request; for example, 200 indicates that everything is okay, 301 means a resource has moved permanently, 404 means the resource is missing, and 500 signifies that there's been an error.[3] By default, Sinatra will send a status code of 200, but you can set it manually using the **status** method in a route handler; for example:

```
get '/fake-error' do
  status 500
  "There's nothing wrong, really :P"
end
```

# Instance Variables

We've already seen how we can place logic in the views, but we can also place it inside the route handlers. How do we share values from the handler with the view? The answer is instance variables!

Instance variables are always preceded by the @ symbol, as in the following examples:

```
@name = "DAZ"
@title = "Jump Start Sinatra"
```

---

[3] See http://en.wikipedia.org/wiki/List_of_HTTP_status_codes for a more comprehensive list.

These work in a similar way to normal variables, but are also accessible in the view; so if an instance variable is set in the handler, it can be referred to in the associated view.

Here's a basic example to illustrate the point:

```
require 'sinatra'
get '/instance' do
  @name = "DAZ"
  erb :show
end
__END__
@@show
<h1>Hello <%= @name %>!</h1>
```

The instance variable @name is set in the route handler and then used to display the name as a heading in the view. If a standard variable of name is used, it is only available in the route handler itself and would show an error if we tried to refer to it in the view.

We're going to use instance variables to set a title for each page. To do this, we'll edit the layout file:

chapter02/views/layout.erb *(excerpt)*

```
<!doctype html>
<html lang="en">
<head>
  <title><%= @title || "Songs By Sinatra" %></title>   ❶
  ⋮
  <header>
    <h1>Songs By Sinatra</h1>   ❷
```

❶  This line is the important one, where we use an instance variable in the title, as well as ERB to display the content from the @title instance variable. If this variable is nil (because it hasn't been set in the route handler), the "Songs By Sinatra" string will be displayed as a default title.

❷  We remove the title variable that we were previously using.

To use this approach, let's add a @title instance variable to the /about route in **main.rb**:

chapter02/main.rb *(excerpt)*

```ruby
get '/about' do
  @title = "All About This Website"
  erb :about
end
```

Now if you navigate to http://localhost:4567/about, you should see that the title has been set to "All About This Website." Have a go at setting the `@title` in the other route handlers, too!

# Start Your Engines

So far, we've been using ERB to produce our views, but there are actually a large number of engines that can render HTML in Sinatra using the Tilt interface. At the time of writing, Sinatra supports the following rendering engines:

| | |
|---|---|
| **Haml** | http://haml.info/ |
| **ERB** | http://ruby-doc.org/stdlib/libdoc/erb/rdoc/ERB.html |
| **Liquid** | http://liquidmarkup.org/ |
| **Markdown** | http://daringfireball.net/projects/markdown/ |
| **Textile** | http://www.textism.com/tools/textile/ |
| **Radius** | http://radius.rubyforge.org/ |
| **Markaby (Markup as Ruby)** | http://markaby.rubyforge.org/ |
| **Slim** | http://slim-lang.com/ |

I'm a big fan of Slim as it reads just like HTML, but without any of the angle brackets and closing tags. Slim uses indentation to avoid closing brackets. Take, for example, the following HTML:

```html
<!doctype html>
<html lang="en">
  <head>
    <title><%= @title || "Songs By Sinatra" %></title>
    <meta charset="utf-8">
    <link rel="stylesheet" href="styles.css">
  </head>
  <body>
    <header>
      <h1>Songs By Sinatra</h1>
```

In Slim, this would be written as:

```
doctype html
html lang="en"
  head
    title= @title || "Songs By Sinatra"
    meta charset="utf-8"
    link rel="stylesheet" href="/styles.css"
  body
    header
      h1 Songs By Sinatra
```

Notice how it looks a lot tidier and easier to read without all those angle brackets? Ruby can also be embedded in Slim files in much the same way as ERB. A hyphen [-] is used to start blocks of logic that are not to be displayed:

```
- name = '<h1>DAZ</h1>'
```

An equals sign, [=], is used for Ruby that's to be evaluated and sent to the browser:

```
= name
```

This will be sent back as escaped HTML, so for this snippet the browser would display the full string "<h1>DAZ</h1>". This can be useful if you want to show the HTML code, or if you lack control over the code that's being displayed and want to safeguard against any nasty HTML being injected into a page.

If you don't want the HTML to be escaped, use the double equals ==:

```
== name
```

This would display the string "DAZ" as a level-one heading in the browser. Slim has a number of other handy features that you can find in the online documentation.[4]

For the rest of the book, I'll be using Slim rather than ERB for the views. Before we do that, we need to make sure that the slim gem is installed:

```
$ gem install slim
```

---

[4] http://rdoc.info/github/stonean/slim

Next, we need to change the method calls from `erb` to `slim` in **main.rb**:

*chapter02/main.rb (excerpt)*

```ruby
require 'sinatra'
require 'slim'

get '/' do
  slim :home
end

get '/about' do
  @title = "All About This Website"
  slim :about
end

get '/contact' do
  slim :contact
end

not_found do
  slim :not_found
end
```

Now all the views need their file extension changed to **.slim** and the content changed to Slim from the original ERB:

*chapter02/views/layout.slim (excerpt)*

```slim
doctype html
html lang="en"
  head
    title== @title || "Songs By Sinatra"
    meta charset="utf-8"
    link rel="stylesheet" href="/styles.css"
  body
    header
      h1 Songs By Sinatra
      nav
        ul
          li <a href="/" title="Home">Home</a>
          li <a href="/about" title="About">About</a>
          li <a href="/contact" title="Contact">Contact</a>
    section
      == yield
```

chapter02/views/home.slim *(excerpt)*

```
p Welcome to this website that's all about the songs of the great F
➥rank Sinatra.
img src="/images/sinatra.jpg" alt="Frank Sinatra"
```

chapter02/views/about.slim *(excerpt)*

```
p This site is a demonstration of how to build a website using Sina
➥tra.
```

chapter02/views/contact.slim *(excerpt)*

```
p You can contact me by sending an email to daz at gmail.com
```

chapter02/views/not_found.slim *(excerpt)*

```
h2 4 Oh 4!
p The page you are looking for is missing. Why not go back to the
➥  <a href='/'>home page</a> and start over?
```

# Partials

One last point to note about views is that they can be nested inside one another. You might like to take a large part of the view logic out into a separate view, perhaps to tidy it up or reuse it. These parts are often known as **partials**. To use a partial, you simply call the name of it from within a view. For example, if we wanted to place the navigation view in a separate partial, we could change **layout.slim** to:

chapter02/views/layout.slim *(excerpt)*

```
doctype html
html lang="en"
  head
    title== @title || "Songs By Sinatra"
    meta charset="utf-8"
    link rel="stylesheet" href="/styles.css"
  body
    header
      h1 Songs By Sinatra
```

```
    == slim :nav
  section
    == yield
```

We'd then have to create another view file called **nav.slim** containing this code:

```
nav
  ul
    li <a href="/" title="Home">Home</a>
    li <a href="/about" title="About">About</a>
    li <a href="/contact" title="Contact">Contact</a>
```

# Getting Sassy

CSS preprocessors have become very popular recently as they add a lot of powerful features to the usual CSS hallmarks, such as variables and mixins. The preprocessor **variables** allow you to assign CSS declarations to variables that can then be reused and finally evaluated in your CSS. For example, you may reuse a color keyword or hexadecimal value assigned to a variable. A **mixin** reuses fragments of CSS containing properties or selectors that can be included in other declarations. This helps to keep your CSS DRY, as you only need to write the code once in the mixin.

Two of the most popular CSS preprocessors around at the moment are Sass[5] and LESS.[6] Sass comes in two flavors: original Sass and the more recent SCSS, which is even closer to CSS. As usual, Sinatra makes it incredibly easy to use either of these. We're going to focus on using the SCSS flavor of Sass in this book, but if you're more familiar with one of the others, you should have no problem with those alternatives. To start using Sass, we first have to install the **sass** gem:

```
$ gem install sass
```

We should also ensure that we `require` this gem at the top of **main.rb**:

---

[5] http://sass-lang.com/
[6] http://lesscss.org/

chapter02/main.rb *(excerpt)*

```
require 'sass'
```

We'll be creating a **styles.scss** file in the **views** folder shortly, so let's create a route handler for it. Place the following bit of code before your other route handlers in **main.rb** (I prefer to keep it at the top of the file):

chapter02/main.rb *(excerpt)*

```
get('/styles.css'){ scss :styles }
```

This is a simple route handler that uses the `scss` to process the `styles` view when the **styles.css** file is requested (there are similar Sass and LESS methods if you prefer to use a different CSS preprocessor). You may have noticed that this route handler looks a bit different from those that we've used previously. This is just a slightly different way of defining a block in Ruby. Usually, they start with `do` and finish with `end`, with all the logic in-between; however, if they fit on one line, it is idiomatic to place the logic inside curly braces, { … }. Hence, this type of route handler is often used for one liners.

Finally, to make this work, we also have to delete the **styles.css** file from the public folder; otherwise, it will take precedence over the `scss` view (all public folder files are displayed before any route handlers with the same URL).

Then we create an SCSS file, which is saved in the views folder, rather than the public folder. Save the following as **styles.scss** in the **views** folder:

chapter02/views/styles.scss

```
$red: #903;
$black: #444;
$white: #fff;
$main-font: Helvetica, Arial, sans-serif;

body {
  font-family: $main-font;
}

h1 {
  color: $red;
```

```scss
    font: 32px/1 $main-font;
}

header h1 {
  font-size: 40px;
  line-height: 80px;
  background: transparent url(/images/logo.png) 0 0 no-repeat;
  padding-left: 84px;
}

@mixin tabs ($background: blue, $color: yellow) {
  ul {
    list-style: none;
    margin: 0;
    padding: 0;
    background: $background;
    overflow: hidden;
  }
  li {
    float: left;
  }
  a {
    text-decoration: none;
    display: block;
    padding: 8px;
    background: $background;
    color: $color;
    &:hover {
      background: darken($background, 20%);
    }
  }
}

nav {
  @include tabs ($background: $black, $color: $white);
  font-weight: bold;
}

p {
  font: 13px/1.4 $main-font;
}
```

This example uses variables to store the colors and names of fonts as a variable at the top of the file:

```
$red: #903;
$black: #444;
$white: #fff;
$main-font: Helvetica, Arial, sans-serif;
```

This is really useful because if we decide later that we want a different shade of red, we only need to change the color code in one place.

After the variables is a mixin for making an unordered list of links look like tabs:

```
@mixin tabs ($background: blue, $color: yellow) {
  ul {
    list-style: none;
    margin: 0;
    padding: 0;
    background: $background;
    overflow: hidden;
  }
  li {
    float: left;
  }
  a {
    text-decoration: none;
    display: block;
    padding: 8px;
    background: $background;
    color: $color;
    &:hover {
      background: darken($background, 20%);
    }
  }
}
```

This mixin has two arguments: the background of the tabs and the color we use for the font, which default to blue and yellow respectively. These defaults can be changed when the mixin is used, as we'll see soon (let's face it, who wants blue and yellow tabs?).

The mixin is applied to the nav element, so that any of the elements mentioned in the mixin appearing as children of the nav will have those styles applied to them:

```
nav {
  @include tabs ($background: $black, $color: $white);
  font-weight: bold;
}
```

And that's it! If you restart the server and take a look in your browser, it should look like Figure 2.6.

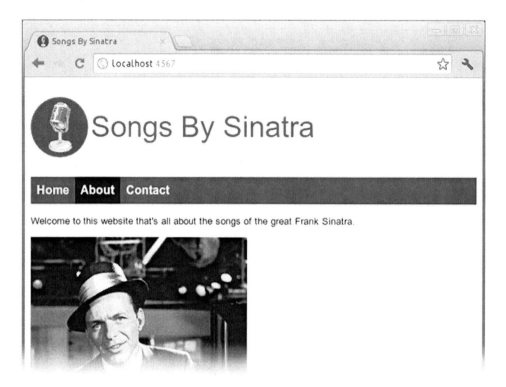

Figure 2.6. Adding some Sass

# Take the Long View

We have covered a lot of ground in this chapter, learning how views work in Sinatra. We've managed to create a simple site with routes, error pages, and styles. The amount of code used to get this site up and running was fairly minimal, so I trust you're starting to see how Sinatra and Slim make a lean combination.

# Collecting Records

In the last chapter, we built a fully functioning website. We covered external views, used the Slim templating engine, and created styles with Sass.

In this chapter, we'll look at storing some of our data in a database. We will create a Song class and use it to populate a database of songs. We'll learn how to create, read, update, and delete songs in the database, and then develop a web front end to accomplish this.

## Databases

If we are going to build a dynamic website, we need a place to store the page information. A database is for keeping data organized. In a traditional relational database, the data is organized into rows that form tables. Each row represents an item in the database, and each column represents a property. Typically, each item in the database is given an ID value that uniquely identifies it; this is usually an integer that increases by one for each subsequent item added to the database. An example of some rows in a typical relational database can be seen in Table 3.1.

Table 3.1. Example Database

| id | forename | surname | age |
|----|----------|---------|-----|
| 1 | "Bart" | "Simpson" | 10 |
| 2 | "Lisa" | "Simpson" | 8 |
| 3 | "Maggie" | "Simpson" | 1 |

There are a number of popular databases that can be used for web development. These include MySQL, SQL Server, PostgreSQL, SQLite, and Oracle. They all use slightly different interpretations of Structured Query Language (SQL) to interact with the database. One of the easiest to use on a local machine is SQLite.

# Installing SQLite

SQLite is an open-source project that stores data in a single file. This means that there's no complicated setup procedure and no need to start a database server.

## Windows

Go to the SQLite download page[1] and download the following packages:

- sqlite-shell
- sqlite-dll

Save these into the folder **C:\WINDOWS\system32**.

After you've done this, install the SQLite Ruby driver gem:

```
$ gem install sqlite
```

## GNU/Linux

On Debian-based systems, you need to install the following packages:

- sqlite3
- libsqlite3-dev

Alternatively, you can install by compiling it directly from the source.

---

[1] http://www.sqlite.org/download.html#win32

Once complete, install the SQLite Ruby driver gem:

```
$ gem install sqlite
```

## Mac OS X

The easiest way to grab the latest version of SQLite is to use Homebrew:

```
$ brew install sqlite
```

You'll then have to install the SQLite Ruby driver gem:

```
$ gem install sqlite
```

 **Nonrelational Databases**

There has been a recent explosion of interest in nonrelational databases that use a different data structure to model information such as graphs, objects, documents, and key-value stores, instead of tables. They also tend not to use SQL to interact with the data. They attempt to solve some of the problems that arise when using traditional relational databases, particularly with storing large amounts of data.

Some of the most popular at the moment are Redis,[2] CouchDB,[3] DynamoDB,[4] MongoDB,[5] and Neo4j.[6] The good news is that Sinatra supports all of them. It's an exciting time in database development and these are well worth checking out.

# Object Relational Mappers

As we've established, SQL databases store data in tables and rows, whereas Ruby has objects with properties. Ruby objects, however, don't map exactly to database tables, although the two are similar. **Object Relational Mappers (ORMs)** perform this mapping for you by ironing out any small differences in the background. This has many advantages: normally you write less code as all the common requirements are taken care of transparently. It also makes your code database-agnostic; so, for

[2] http://redis.io/
[3] http://couchdb.apache.org/
[4] http://aws.amazon.com/dynamodb/
[5] http://www.mongodb.org/
[6] http://neo4j.org/

instance, you could change from using SQLite to PostgreSQL without having to change any of your code. This is a good separation between the business logic of your app and the persistence of its data.

Roughly speaking, each Ruby class will be represented by a table in the database, and every instance of that class will be represented by a row in the table. The object's properties will be the columns.

There are a number of popular ORM options in Sinatra, including Active Record,[7] DataMapper,[8] and Sequel.[9]

## DataMapper

DataMapper is a relatively new entrant into the ORM stable, but is already a popular option and fits well with Sinatra. It's written in Ruby and has a really simple syntax that's easy to come to grips with while allowing you to manipulate the data in your database with ease.

All the data interactions are written in Ruby and don't require you to get your hands dirty writing any SQL statements (a definite plus—believe me!).

Installing DataMapper is easy; being a Ruby gem, all that's required is to type the following line into a command prompt:

```
$ gem install data_mapper
```

Since we'll be using SQLite, we also need to install the adapter for it:

```
$ gem install dm-sqlite-adapter
```

## Song Class

We're going to devise a Song class that will allow us to create and save information about songs by Frank Sinatra to a database. Start a new file called **song.rb** with the following require statements:

---

[7] http://rubygems.org/gems/activerecord
[8] http://datamapper.org/
[9] http://sequel.rubyforge.org/

*chapter03/song.rb (excerpt)*

```
require 'dm-core'
require 'dm-migrations'
```

The first gem, dm-core, is the main DataMapper gem. dm-migrations is an extension that we'll use later to give us extra functionality. Next, we need to connect to the database using the following line of code:

*chapter03/song.rb (excerpt)*

```
DataMapper.setup(:default, "sqlite3://#{Dir.pwd}/development.db")
```

This will create a file called **development.db** (if it doesn't already exist), which will store all the database information. All we do now is create our Song class in Ruby:

*chapter03/song.rb (excerpt)*

```
class Song
  include DataMapper::Resource ❶
  property :id, Serial ❷
  property :title, String ❸
  property :lyrics, Text ❹
  property :length, Integer ❺
  property :released_on, Date ❻
end

DataMapper.finalize ❼
```

❶   The line include DataMapper::Resource links the Song class to DataMapper, which includes the Resource module from the DataMapper gem as a mixin. This is how you make any Ruby class a DataMapper resource.

 **DataMapper Properties**

After this line, we list the properties of the Song class. DataMapper properties all have a type, which normally correspond to Ruby core classes. Here are some common examples:

**String**    is used for short text strings (up to a maximum of 256 characters)
**Text**    is used for longer pieces of text
**Integer**    is used for whole numbers

**Float**       is used for floating point numbers
**Boolean**     is used for true or false values
**DateTime**    is used for dates and times

**2** Our `:id` uses a special type called Serial, which gives each song an identifier that auto-increments.

**3** The `:title` is used to store short song titles, which means a string is fine.

**4** As the lyrics could end up being longer than 256 characters for some songs, we'll use the text type for `:lyrics`.

**5** `:length` stores the length of the song in seconds, so we can store this as an integer (we can convert it into minutes and seconds manually if we wish).

**6** `:released_on` keeps a record of the date of release. The most convenient way to store such information is by using Ruby's built-in `Date` class.

**7** The `DataMapper.finalize` method is required after all classes using DataMapper to check their integrity. It needs to be called before the app starts interacting with any classes. We only have one `Song` class at the moment, so it can just go at the end of this class definition.

# Interacting with the Song Class in IRB

Interactive Ruby (IRB) allows you to enter Ruby code one line at a time and receive real-time feedback. It's great for experimenting with Ruby, which is why we're going to use it to interact with the `Song` class that we just created. We'll concoct some song objects and then save them to the database.

To launch IRB, open up a terminal and navigate to the folder that contains the file **song.rb**. Now enter the following command:

```
$ irb
```

You should see a prompt similar to the following:

```
irb(main):001:0>
```

 **IRB Prompt**

In the interests of economy, from here on when we refer to the IRB prompt, we'll state it as follows:

```
irb>
```

Next, we need to require the file **song.rb**, so that the Song class is available to IRB:

```
irb> require './song'
=> true
```

## Migrations

DataMapper has a brilliant plugin called automigrations. This basically takes the properties listed in the Ruby class and creates the relevant table and columns for you. This is the first task before we can start interacting with the database:

```
irb> Song.auto_migrate!
=> true
```

The first time we run this command, it should bring up a new file called **development.db** in the same directory as **song.rb**. It will have also created a table called song in the database with the relevant columns for each property.

# CRUD Operations

Now we are able to interact with the Song class. There are four standard operations that you can apply to database tables: Create, Read, Update, and Delete. These are commonly known as the CRUD operations. DataMapper makes it easy to carry out these operations using its simple Ruby syntax. We'll do this in IRB initially, as it offers a convenient way of applying the four CRUD operations using the methods that DataMapper makes available to us.

## Creating Songs

Let's start by adding a new song:

```
irb> song = Song.new
=> #<Song @id=nil @title=nil @lyrics=nil @length=nil @released_on=ni
➥1>
```

You can see that a Song object has been created, but all the properties are nil because they're yet to be set. At the moment, this object is only stored in memory; it hasn't been saved to the database. That's easy to do:

```
irb> song.save
=> true
```

If we take a look at what the Song object looks like now, we'll see that the id property has been set to 1:

```
irb> song
=> #<Song @id=1 @title=nil @lyrics=nil @length=nil @released_on=nil>
```

This is the auto-increment feature of the Serial type taking effect—every new object saved to the database will have an id that's one more than the previous entry. The other properties are still nil, so let's change that:

```
irb> song.title = "My Way"
```

```
irb> song.lyrics = "And now the end is near ... "
```

```
irb> song.length = 435
```

```
irb> song.released_on = Date.new(1969)
```

```
irb> song.save
```

We've now saved all the relevant information about our first song to the database. However, there's actually a more convenient way of creating a resource in one line by using the create method:

```
irb> Song.create(title: "Come Fly With Me", lyrics: "Come fly with m
➥e, let's fly, let's fly away ... .", length: 199, released_on: Dat
➥e.new(1958,1,6))
```

This will create and save the song all in one go. We should now have two songs saved in the database. We can see check this by using the count method:

```
irb> Song.count
=> 2
```

# Reading Songs

If we want to read the properties of a particular song, or group of songs, we need to be able to find them in the database. The easiest way to retrieve them is all at once:

```
irb> Song.all
=> [#<Song @id=1 @title="My Way" @lyrics=<not loaded> @length=435 @
➥released_on=#<Date: 1969-1-1>>, #<Song @id=2 @title="Come Fly With
➥Me" @lyrics=<not loaded> @length=199 @released_on =#<Date: 1958-1-
➥6>>]
```

This returns all the songs created so far and stores them in an array. You can then perform any array operations on it, such as reversing the order:

```
irb> Song.all.reverse
=> [#<Song @id=2 @title="Come Fly With Me" @lyrics=<not loaded> @le
➥ngth=199 @released_on=#<Date: 1958-1-6>>,#<Song @id=1 @title="My W
➥ay" @lyrics=<not loaded> @length=435 @released_on =#<Date: 1969-1-
➥1>>]
```

If we only want the first song in the database, there are a few ways of doing this:

```
irb> Song.get(1)
=> #<Song @id=1 @title="My Way" @lyrics=<not loaded> @length=435 @r
➥eleased_on=#<Date: 1969-1-1>>
```

This will get the song with an id of 1, which is useful if we know the specific ID of an object (1 in this case). If we just want to find the first entry, we can use the first method:

```
irb> Song.first
=> #<Song @id=1 @title="My Way" @lyrics=<not loaded> @length=435 @r
➥eleased_on=#<Date: 1969-1-1>>
```

In a similar way, we can find the last song:

```
irb> Song.last
=> #<Song @id=2 @title="Come Fly With Me" @lyrics=<not loaded> @len
➥gth=199 @released_on=#<Date: 1958-1-6>>
```

We can also narrow down our search by adding some attributes by which to query. For example, we might want to find the song that has the title of "My Way." This is easily done using the following query:

```
irb> myway = Song.first(title: "My Way")
=> #<Song @id=1 @title="My Way" @lyrics=<not loaded> @length=435 @re
➥leased_on=#<Date: 1969-1-1>>
```

## Updating Songs

In the previous code example, we found the first song with a title of "My Way" and stored it in the variable myway. We can find out the length of the song in seconds by querying its length method:

```
irb> myway.length
=> 435
```

This is actually incorrect. The length of the song is 4 minutes and 35 seconds. Our length property is stored in seconds, so it should say 275. We can correct it by using the update method:

```
irb> myway.update(length: 275)
=> true
```

Using the update method will change the length property to 275 and then save it to the database. We can verify that it has in fact been updated by querying the length value again:

```
irb> myway.length
=> 275
```

Now everything is correct!

## Deleting Songs

Deleting songs is easy to do using the `destroy` method. To demonstrate this, I'm going to create a sacrificial song:

```
irb> Song.create(title: "One Less Lonely Girl")
=> #<Song @id=3 @title="One Less Lonely Girl" @lyrics=nil @length=ni
➥l @released_on=nil>
```

Clearly this song is not what Ol' Blue Eyes would sing, so we'll delete it:

```
irb> Song.last.destroy
=> true
```

This example shows how we can chain some of DataMapper's methods together. First of all, we used the `last` method to find the last song in the list (the one we just added); then we immediately called the `destroy` method on that song. Let's just check that it has been deleted by ensuring that the last song in our database is "Come Fly With Me" rather than "One Less Lonely Girl":

```
irb> Song.last
=> #<Song @id=2 @title="Come Fly With Me" @lyrics=<not loaded> @len
➥gth=199 @released_on=#<Date: 1958-1-6>>
```

Perfect!

# Putting It on the Web

We now have a fully functioning `Song` class, and our song objects are being saved as rows in our database table. We now have to create a web front end to perform these operations. This is where Sinatra comes in. In fact, this is what Sinatra is all about—connecting Ruby to the Web!

If you were yet to notice, our current **song.rb** file doesn't use Sinatra at all. This is to emphasize that it's just a plain old Ruby program. As I mentioned in the section called "What is Sinatra?" in Chapter 1, Sinatra is simply used to connect Ruby programs to the Web using HTTP requests and responses. For Sinatra to be involved, we need to `require` the **song.rb** file in our **main.rb** file from Chapter 2. Make sure that **song.rb** is saved in the same directory as **main.rb**, and add this line to the top of **main.rb**:

chapter03/main.rb (excerpt)

```
require './song'
```

Now we just need to create some route handlers and views to deal with our songs.

# HTTP Verbs

We saw in the section called "What is Sinatra?" in Chapter 1 that the Web is built around the HyperText Transfer Protocol, or HTTP. When a client (usually a browser) makes a request to the server, it contains information about which HTTP verb to use. An HTTP verb tells the server what type of request is being made, which determines how the server deals with the request.

There are a number of HTTP verbs, but in practice we tend to only use five when dealing with resources on the Web:

- GET requests are used to retrieve resources.

- POST requests are usually employed to create a resource but can actually perform any task.

- PUT requests are used to "upsert," which means it can insert a resource or update it in its entirety.

- PATCH requests make partial updates to a resource.

- DELETE requests are used to delete resources.

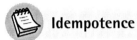 **Idempotence**

When a function is applied multiple times to something, but without changing the result after the first application, it is said to be idempotent. In terms of HTTP methods, this means that a request could be made numerous times, but the result will remain the same after the first successful request. GET, PUT, and DELETE are all expected to be idempotent methods. This means that a browser could theoretically repeat a request if it suspected the first had failed and could expect the same results, even if it ends up that both requests are processed. POST requests, on the other hand, are not idempotent and can change a resource (or several) by sending the same request repeatedly.

This is the language of HTTP and the vocabulary that Sinatra uses to process routes. You may have noticed that these match almost exactly to the CRUD operations used by databases (with PUT and PATCH covering slightly different implementations of Update). This means that we can use these HTTP verbs to issue particular requests depending on which operation we want to do.

A link always performs a GET request. Forms can be used to perform a GET or POST request. There is a slight problem in that most browsers only support GET and POST out of the box. This can be overcome by sending a POST request, and using hidden form fields or JavaScript to send extra information about what the actual request should be to the server, as we'll see later.

Sinatra excels at making these verbs easily accessible through route handlers. In fact, the HTTP verbs are at the start of every route handler, making them central to the way in which Sinatra handles requests. We've already used the GET verb in our previous examples; now it's time to make use of the others.

## RESTful URLs

We're now going to create some route handlers and views to allow us to perform the CRUD operations via a web interface. We'll do this following the REpresentational State Transfer (REST for short) pattern that was first proposed by Roy Fielding in 2000, and is now a popular way of creating URLs on the Web. This basically states that the URL should represent a resource (in this case, the songs in our database). When the URL is requested, a representation of that resource is returned in the response. This representation is typically a web page containing information about that resource.

RESTful URLs are characteristically short and descriptive; because they describe a specific resource, they should contain nouns. What you want to do with the resource ("get" it or "delete" it, for example) is described by the verbs you use, or, more precisely, the HTTP verbs we saw before! If you want to know more about REST, this article by Ryan Tomayko is very informative.[10]

A common pattern, popularized by the Ruby on Rails framework, is that each resource should have the following URLs:

- a list URL that displays all the resources; for example, /songs

- a show URL that shows an individual resource; for example, /songs/2

- a new URL where you can enter the information for a new resource; for example, /songs/new

- a create URL that will actually create new resource; for example, /songs

- an edit view where you can update the information about a resource; for example, /songs/2/edit

- an update URL that will actually update the resource; for example, /songs/2

- a delete URL that will remove a resource; for example, /songs/2

One aspect to notice with this approach is that a number of view, update, and delete operations all have the same URL (/songs/2 in the examples just shown). The operation that's carried out is purely determined by the HTTP verb used. For example, the URL /song/2 will show the song if it's a GET request, but update the song if it's a PUT request. I hope this demonstrates how HTTP verbs and RESTful URLs work together in tandem, as shown in Figure 3.1.

---

[10] http://tomayko.com/writings/rest-to-my-wife

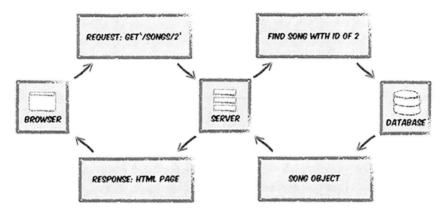

Figure 3.1. The Request and Response Cycle in action

We're going to follow this RESTful pattern for our Song resource. This means that we will have to create a route handler for each URL in the pattern. You will notice that we'll just use all the same DataMapper methods in the route handlers as we used when performing the CRUD operations in IRB; the only difference is that we'll also show a view so that you can see the outcome of any actions.

# Listing Songs

Our first route will simply list all the songs. Add the following route handler to the bottom of **song.rb**:

```
                                                    chapter03/song.rb (excerpt)

get '/songs' do
  @songs = Song.all
  slim :songs
end
```

The route handler will need to find all the song records in the database. We'll store this in an instance variable called @songs, as it will allow us to access it in the view. After we've done this, we finish by displaying the relevant view, called :songs. Next, we need to create that view, which will be saved in the **views** folder:

```
                                              chapter03/views/songs.slim

h1 Songs
a href="/songs/new" Create a new song
- if @songs.any?
```

```
ul#songs
  -@songs.each do |song|
    li <a href="/songs/#{song.id}">#{song.title}</a>
- else
  p No songs have been created yet!
```

We start with a heading and a link to create a new song, which we'll use later. Then we check to see if there are any songs stored in the instance variable @songs. If there are, we iterate through them all and display a link to the page that shows the song information, which is what we'll sort out next! Run `ruby main.rb` to see the page shown in Figure 3.2.

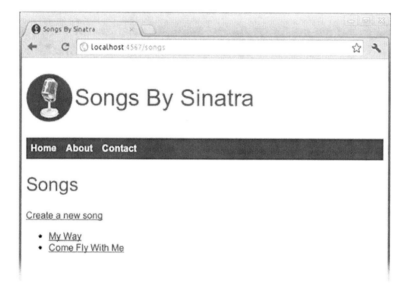

Figure 3.2. Listing the songs

## Showing Songs

If we have created all these songs, we're going to want to see them! For this, we will need to find the song and display the relevant information in a view. Here's a route handler to achieve it:

chapter03/song.rb *(excerpt)*

```
get '/songs/:id' do
  @song = Song.get(params[:id])
  slim :show_song
end
```

First of all, we find the relevant song from the :id variable that's in the URL and stored in the *params* hash. This is stored in an instance variable, @song, so we can access it in the view **show_song.slim**:

chapter03/views/show_song.slim

```
h1= @song.title ❶
p Release Date: #{@song.released_on.strftime("%e %B %Y") if @song.re
➥leased_on} ❷
p Length: #{@song.length/60} minutes #{@song.length%60} seconds ❸
pre= @song.lyrics ❹
p <a href="/songs">back to songs index</a> ❺
p <a href="/songs/#{@song.id}/edit">edit this song</a> ❻
form action="/songs/#{@song.id}" method="POST" ❼
  input type="hidden" name="_method" value="DELETE" ❽
  input type="submit" value="delete this song"
```

❶  This view shows the title of the song as a level-one heading.

❷  For the release date, we use the strftime method to format the date object that's returned from the database into a more readable format of day, month, and year.

 **The strftime Method**

strftime is an unusually named Ruby method that can be used on dates to format them. It uses directives that begin with a percent [%] character to show different parts of the date. For example, if you want the name of the month in full (that is, "January") you would use the directive %B. If you only wanted the abbreviated month (that is, "Jan"), you would use the directive %b. You can also insert any plain text into the string and it will be displayed with the date information. Here's an example that you can try in IRB:

```
Time.now.strftime("Today is day %e of the month of %B in th
➥e year of %Y")
=> "Today is day  9 of the month of October in the year of
2012"
```

For more information about the unusual notation of the `strftime` method, see http://foragoodstrftime.com/.

❸ The song length is stored in the database as an integer that represents the number of seconds the song lasts. To find the number of minutes, we divide it by 60 (integer division in Ruby ignores any remainders); to find the number of seconds remaining, we use the modulo operator %.

❹ The lyrics are displayed inside <pre> tags to preserve any formatting.

❺ After the lyrics, there is a link back to the list of songs that we created in the last section.

❻ This is a link to edit the song, which we'll deal with later.

❼ The last part of this view is a form that contains a button to delete the song from the database.

❽ We need a form so that we can use a DELETE request, which is achieved by adding the hidden input field with the attributes of `name="_method"` and `value="DELETE"`. Deleting songs will be covered later.

The view should look like Figure 3.3.

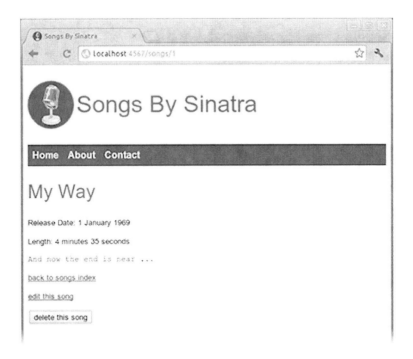

Figure 3.3. Showing a song

## Creating New Songs

Now we'll develop a route that will allow us to create a new song. This uses two routes; one shows the form for creating the song while the other actually creates the song. The first is the page where we enter the information:

```
                                              chapter03/song.rb (excerpt)

get '/songs/new' do
  @song = Song.new
  slim :new_song
end

get '/songs/:id' do
  @song = Song.get(params[:id])
  slim :show_song
end
```

This route handler simply creates an empty Song object and then displays the new_song view, which we now need to create and save in the views folder:

chapter03/views/new_song.slim

```
h1 Add A New Song
form method="POST" action="/songs"
  == slim :song_form
```

This is a simple view that starts with a form tag, but then uses a nested view called **song_form**. Because we'll be using the same form for creating a new song as for editing a song, it makes sense to keep the form fields in a separate, reusable file. The start of the form is slightly different in both cases as the action attribute contains a different URL, so this needs to be in the **new_song** view. Here's the code for the form fields:

chapter03/views/song_form.slim

```
label for="title" Title:
input#title type="text" name="song[title]" value="#{@song.title}"
label for="length" Length:
input#length type="number" name="song[length]" value="#{@song.lengt
➥h}"
label for="released_on" Date(mm/dd/yyyy):
input#released_on type="text" name="so
➥ng[released_on]" value="#{@song.released_on.strftime("%m/%d/%Y") i
➥f @song.released_on}"
label for="lyrics" Lyrics:
textarea#lyrics name="song[lyrics]" == @song.lyrics
input type="submit" value="Save Song"
```

Notice that the name attribute of the input fields all specify the name of the class (song), followed by the property in square brackets (song[title], for example). It specifies what property that field relates to, and a hash will be created called params[:song] that contains all the values entered in the form. This means that we can create a new song by just using the line Song.create(params[:song]), rather than having to mention each property individually. The value of each field is also set to the value of the @song object. As this is a new Song object, all the values are nil, as seen in Figure 3.4; however, when we reuse this form later for editing songs, the current values are displayed in the relevant fields.

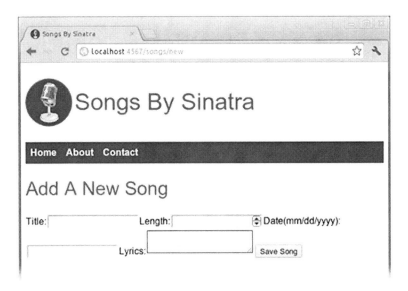

Figure 3.4. Adding a new song

There is a slight catch, though, because the `released_on` property is a date. The value entered in the form is just a string in the format mm/dd/yyyy. DataMapper expects it to be a Ruby Date object. There isn't a way to enter a date in this format via a form, so we need to add a little method to the `Song` class that will perform the conversion for us.

Edit the `Song` class so it looks like the code below:

chapter03/song.rb *(excerpt)*

```
class Song
  include DataMapper::Resource
  property :id, Serial
  property :title, String
  property :lyrics, Text
  property :length, Integer
  property :released_on, Date

  def released_on=date
    super Date.strptime(date, '%m/%d/%Y')
  end
end
```

The `released_on=` method at the end will use the values entered in the `released_on` field and convert them into a Date object. This can then be used by the database.

When the form is submitted, the `action` attribute specifies that it should be sent using a POST request to the URL /create/song, so let's create a route handler:

```
                                                    chapter03/song.rb (excerpt)
post '/songs' do
  song = Song.create(params[:song])
  redirect to("/songs/#{song.id}")
end
```

Once the new song has been created, we redirect to the new song's URL, which references its `id`; for example, if we had just created a song with an `id` of 2, its URL would be /song/2.

## The Redirect Helper

`redirect` is a helper method that can be used to … well, redirect to another page. It is often used after an action has been carried out, as witnessed with creating new songs. `to` is another helper method that is actually an alias for the `url` method. This is used to generate the correct URL if reverse proxies or namespaces are being used (probably not worth worrying too much about it at the moment, but it's a good idea to become familiar with using the helper anyway, just in case). Because of the clever naming of these helpers, they read very nicely together ("redirect to"). Sinatra has lots more useful helper methods like these that we'll come across in later chapters.

# Editing Songs

Editing songs is similar to creating them. The only difference is that we need to specify the `id` of the song that we wish to edit in the URL. This will then be added to the `params` hash with the key of `:id`. We can use this to query the database and find the relevant song, which is then stored in an instance variable called `@song` so that it can be used in the view:

```
                                          chapter03/song.rb (excerpt)
get '/songs/:id/edit' do
  @song = Song.get(params[:id])
  slim :edit_song
end
```

The associated view is called `edit_song` and needs to be saved in the **views** folder:

```
                                      chapter03/views/edit_song.slim
h1 Edit Song
form method="POST" action="/songs/#{@song.id}"
  input type="hidden" name="_method" value="PUT"
  == slim :song_form
```

Here we make use of the `song_form` view by reusing it, as it has all the same fields as the form we used in the `new_song` view. The only difference is that here we're using a PUT request, although it is actually sent as a POST request, as shown in the form's `method`. Ideally, we'd like to use `method="PUT"`, but this is not supported by most browsers. To overcome this, we can use a hidden `input` field with the `name` and `value` attributes set to `_method` and `PUT` respectively. This tells the server that we want to use a PUT request rather than a POST request; it's also how Sinatra manages to use any HTTP verbs beyond those natively supported by the browser.

When the form is submitted, it goes to the update URL. Here's its route handler:

```
                                          chapter03/song.rb (excerpt)
put '/songs/:id' do
  song = Song.get(params[:id])
  song.update(params[:song])
  redirect to("/songs/#{song.id}")
end
```

We're using a PUT request here because we're updating the whole song object (even if we only changed one of the properties, the whole row in the database is updated and saved again). The route handler finds the relevant song using the `id` attribute in the URL that's stored in the `params` hash. We update the song object using the values stored in the `params[:song]` hash using DataMapper's `update` method. We then redirect to the song's URL so that the edits can be seen, as in Figure 3.5.

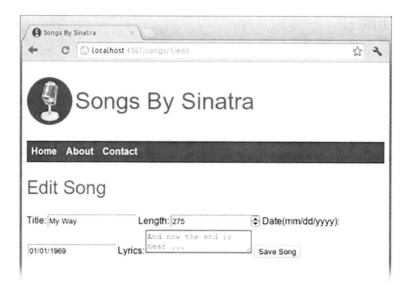

Figure 3.5. Editing a song

## Deleting Songs

Last of all, we want to be able to delete any songs that are no longer required in the database. The actual button to delete the song can be found on the song's show page in this bit of code:

```
                                chapter03/views/show_song.slim (excerpt)
form action="/songs/#{@song.id}" method="POST"
   input type="hidden" name="_method" value="DELETE"
   input type="submit" value="delete this song"
```

This code uses a form to create a button so that a `hidden input` field can tell the server that we're actually making a DELETE request, rather than a POST request.

To delete the song, we locate the relevant song and use DataMapper's `destroy` method to remove it:

```
                                        chapter03/song.rb (excerpt)
delete '/songs/:id' do
   Song.get(params[:id]).destroy
   redirect to('/songs')
end
```

This handler uses a DELETE request, so we know that its function is to remove a resource. We find the song and call the `destroy` method all in one line. Then we redirect to the list of songs page to reveal the new list without the deleted song.

# Finishing Touches

Now we'll edit the **nav.slim** file to add a link to the songs section of our website. Edit the navigation list in **nav.slim** to look like the following:

chapter03/views/nav.slim *(excerpt)*

```
li <a href="/" title="Home">Home</a>
li <a href="/about" title="About">About</a>
li <a href="/contact" title="Contact">Contact</a>
li <a href="/songs" title="Songs">Songs</a>
```

And finally, a small change that will help improve the look of the form is to make the labels block-level elements, which forces them to start on a new line. This is easily achieved by adding the following line to the bottom of **styles.scss**:

chapter03/views/styles.scss *(excerpt)*

```
label { display: block; }
```

Now we have a fully functioning web front end for our songs! We can see a list of all our songs, view them individually, edit them, create new ones, and delete them. Start your server and have a go at performing each of the CRUD operations.

# For the Record

This chapter has seen us introduce databases into our web application. We installed SQLite and created a `Song` class. We then used DataMapper to perform the CRUD operations to create, read, update, and destroy song records.

We then built a web front end to allow the database to be updated using an online form. We used RESTful URLs to present a list of all songs, show an individual song, create a new song, edit an existing song, and delete a song.

In the next chapter, we'll look at different configuration settings that Sinatra offers us, and deploy our site to the Internet.

# Setting up to Go Live

In the last chapter, we created a Song model and database table to store the songs in. We also created a web front end for creating, reading, editing, and deleting them.

In this chapter, we'll look at the different settings that are available in Sinatra and learn how to configure an application. We'll also address using sessions and discover how they can be employed to create a simple login system. Later, we'll cover deploying our application live on the Internet using the Heroku service.

## Configuration

Any configuration options for a Sinatra application can be set in a `configure` block:

```
configure do
  #configuration options go here
end
```

Code inside this block is run only once at startup. You can have as many `configure` blocks as you like in a Sinatra app and they can be placed at any point in the code, but the accepted convention is to use one block and place it near the start of a file.

An example of configuration being used in our application is with the database settings. Find the following line in **song.rb**:

chapter04/song.rb *(excerpt)*

```
DataMapper.setup(:default, "sqlite3://#{Dir.pwd}/development.db")
```

This should really go in a `configure` block, so let's change it to look like this:

chapter04/song.rb *(excerpt)*

```
configure do
  DataMapper.setup(:default, "sqlite3://#{Dir.pwd}/development.db")
end
```

Don't worry about where this block goes—`configure` blocks can go anywhere in the application file. You can even have more than one `configure` block in different places across the application! The convention is to have just the one `configure` block that comes near the top of the file.

## Environments

All Rack applications, including Sinatra, use the concept of environments to signify the stage of development an application is in. There are three predefined environments: development, production (when your app is live on the server), and test.

Development is the default environment in Sinatra. Template files are automatically reloaded on each request, and there are special "not found" and "error" pages that show a stack trace to help with debugging when there's a problem. You can change the environment when you start the server using the `-e` flag. For example, if we wanted to start the app using the production environment, we'd launch the server by typing:

```
$ ruby main.rb -e production
```

To check what environment the app is running in, the helper methods `production?`, `development?`, and `test?` will return `true` or `false` as appropriate. For example, the following route handler will indicate the environment the app is running in:

```
get '/environment' do
  if development?
    "development"
  elsif production?
    "production"
  elsif test?
    "test"
  else
  "Who knows what environment you're in!"
end
```

In fact, we used one of these methods back in the section called "Your First Sinatra App" in Chapter 1 using the following code snippet:

```
require 'sinatra/reloader' if development?
```

This ensures that the code will be reloaded on a page refresh only in development mode (the application would be way too slow if this happened in production).

## Environmental Configuration

Sinatra makes it possible to set different configuration options depending on the environment. This is done by adding an argument to the `configure` block that specifies the required environment. For example, you could have a separate configure block for each environment, as shown in this code sample:

```
configure :production do
  #production configuration here
end

configure :development do
  #development configuration here
end

configure :test do
  #test configuration here
End
```

This can be very useful when distinct configuration options are needed for different environments. For example, let's update our database settings configuration for development only:

```
configure :development do
  DataMapper.setup(:default, "sqlite3://#{Dir.pwd}/development.db")
end
```

# Settings

Settings are application-wide variables that are stored in the `settings` object, which is accessible throughout the application. There are a number of built-in settings that can be changed, of which some of the more useful ones are presented here:

**:public_folder**

This allows you to set the folder that will contain static files. By default, it is called "public," but it can be changed, for example, to "static":

```
set :public_folder, '/static'
```

**:views**

This enables you to set which folder contains all the external view files. By default, it is called "views," but it can be changed, for example, to "templates":

```
set :views, '/templates'
```

**:static**

This can be used to set whether Sinatra checks in the public directory for static files before examining route handlers for a matching route. The default option is set to `true`, but it can be turned off with the following line of code:

```
disable :static
```

**:root**

This changes the folder that is used as the base of the application. By default, this folder contains the main application file.

**:app_file**

This can be used to set the main application file. It can be useful as it sets the root folder, which, in turn, sets the location of the views and public folders.

Sinatra will always try to figure out what the `app_file` is, but there are few situations where you'd want to change this.

**:port**

This setting is used to establish the port that the application will run on once the web server is started. This is set to 4567 by default, but can be changed like so:

```
set :port, 1234
```

Note that this only works if the server is started by executing the Ruby file (as we've been doing so far), rather than using a rackup file (as we'll do later in the section called "Rack It Up!").

**:show_exceptions**

This shows a backtrace on error pages to help with debugging. It is enabled by default in development mode, but can be turned off with the following code:

```
configure :development do
  disable :show_exceptions
end
```

**:logging**

If this is enabled, all error messages are logged to `STDERR`. By default, it is enabled in classic Sinatra applications (this is the only style we have used so far), but is disabled in modular Sinatra applications (which we'll look at in Chapter 7).

## Custom Settings

It's also possible to create your own custom settings in Sinatra. These can be used for application-wide variables and are stored in the `settings` object. Custom settings can be easily created using the `set` method.

 **Sinatra by Extension**

Custom settings are useful when you create a Sinatra extension (see the section called "External Gems" in Chapter 5) as you can use the `settings` object to provide default settings for the extension. These can then be set to other values from within the main application using the `set` method.

For example, we could create a setting called `name` with the value of `Frank` using the following code:

```
set :name, "Frank"
```

To access this, we just need to use the `settings` object like so:

```
settings.name
```

We can even create dynamic settings using a block:

```
set(:image_folder){ :root + '/images' }
```

This will append **/images** at the end of the path to the root folder, and will update if the root folder changes.

Here's another example:

```
set(:dice_roll){ 1 + rand(5) }
```

This will return a different number every time `settings.dice_roll` is called.

## Enable and Disable

Settings that can only have Boolean `true` or `false` values can also be set using `enable` and `disable` for better readability. For example, instead of:

```
set :logging, true
```

we could write:

```
enable :logging
```

These methods also take multiple arguments, so more than one setting can be set to `true` or `false` at once, for example:

```
disable :logging, :sessions
```

This is typical of many of Sinatra's helper methods. They make the code much more readable, which is always ideal!

## Sessions

HTTP is a **stateless protocol**, which means that each request is independent of others. In other words, each request knows nothing about the previous or next request. One way to overcome this and keep track of one request to the next is to use sessions. Sinatra uses cookie-based sessions by default, so small amounts of information can be stored in a session cookie on the user's machine; this information is then accessible via the `session` hash. Session cookies are destroyed when a user's session finishes by closing the browser, so the information only persists for this duration. Sessions are also signed while in production mode with a randomly generated token to ensure that no one has been tampering with the cookie. This token can be set manually using the following setting:

```
set :session_secret, 'try to make this long and hard to guess'
```

 **The Lowdown on Cookies**

Cookies are small files that are saved locally on the user's computer. There are two types of cookies: session cookies and persistent cookies. Session cookies only last for the term of a session, and are deleted when the user closes the browser. Persistent cookies are kept after a session has finished, so can be used by the server in subsequent sessions.

To get started with sessions, you first have to enable them. It only needs to be done once, so it should go in a configure block, like so:

*chapter04/main.rb (excerpt)*

```
configure do
  enable :sessions
end
```

Now you can get and set information using the `session` hash. Here's a quick example:

```
                                                chapter04/main.rb (excerpt)

get '/set/:name' do
  session[:name] = params[:name]
end
```

This route grabs the name entered in the URL and stores it in the `params` hash, as we've previously done. The problem is that the information in the `params` hash will only be available for that request. By placing this value in the `session` hash, it is now available for all requests. We can create another route handler to test this out:

```
                                                chapter04/main.rb (excerpt)

get '/get/hello' do
  "Hello #{session[:name]}"
end
```

Visit http://localhost:4567/set/Frank, and then http://localhost:4567/get/hello; you should see the message `Hello Frank`.

 **Using Sessions with Sinatra::Reloader**

Sessions won't work on older versions of Sinatra if you're using Sinatra::Reloader. You can fix this by either upgrading your version of Sinatra, or setting the `session_secret` manually.

## Implementing a Simple Login Mechanism

We can use sessions to implement a simple login mechanism on our Songs By Sinatra website. To start with, open up **main.rb** and add the following to the configure block near the top of the page (after the `require` statements):

```
                                                chapter04/main.rb (excerpt)

configure do
  enable :sessions
  set :username, 'frank'
  set :password, 'sinatra'
end
```

This enables sessions, then sets up a `username` and `password`. Next, we need a `login` route handler:

chapter04/main.rb *(excerpt)*

```
get '/login' do
  slim :login
end
```

This is a basic route handler that displays a view called `login`. Let's create that view now. Save the following code in a file called **login.slim** in the **views** directory:

chapter04/views/login.slim

```
form action="/login" method="POST"
  label for="username" Username:
  input#username type="text" name="username"
  label for="password" Password:
  input#password type="password" name="password"
  input type="submit" value="Log In"
```

This is a login form that simply has an `input` field for the username and an `input` field for the password. It is submitted to the same URL, but as a POST request, so we need to create a handler to deal with what happens when the form is submitted. Add the following route handler to **main.rb**:

chapter04/main.rb *(excerpt)*

```
post '/login' do
  if params[:username] == settings.username && params[:password] ==
➥ settings.password
    session[:admin] = true
    redirect to('/songs')
  else
    slim :login
  end
end
```

In this route handler, we check to see if the strings entered in the form (saved in the `params` hash) are the same as the strings in the configure block. If they are, we set `session[:admin]` to `true`. This means that if a user is logged in, there will be a session variable called `admin` set to `true`. We can use this to protect some or all of our routes by adding the following code to the top of a route handler:

```
halt(401,'Not Authorized') unless session[:admin]
```

This uses Sinatra's `halt` method to stop the application dead in its tracks, and if the session variable evaluates to anything other than `true`, it issues a 401 status code with the message "Not Authorized."

For example, if we only wanted people who were logged in to be able to have access to the new songs page, we could change the route handler in **song.rb** to the following:

chapter04/song.rb *(excerpt)*

```
get '/songs/new' do
  halt(401,'Not Authorized') unless session[:admin]
  @song = Song.new
  slim :new_song
end
```

Other candidate routes worth protecting are editing songs, deleting songs, creating songs, and updating songs.

## Logging Out

To log out, we destroy the session variable. This can be done by using the `clear` method for the session object. The following route handler will destroy the session and then redirect the user to the login page:

chapter04/main.rb *(excerpt)*

```
get '/logout' do
  session.clear
  redirect to('/login')
end
```

See if you can (or cannot) perform certain tasks depending on whether you are logged in or not. It's a very basic system but it works, and with very little code!

### Beware Session-based Authentication

Being a modest login system, this session-based authentication is certainly not meant to be used in a production setting. If you need a proper authorization system, you should try looking at some of the many gems that are available, such as `sinatra-authentication` or `warden`. Even then, using sessions for authentication can still leave the application vulnerable to, for example, a CSRF (cross-site request forgery) attack.[1] Sinatra does its best to protect against these attacks, but a better solution would be to avoid using session-based authentication altogether and send a token in the HTTP header.

# Deploying the Site

We're now at the stage of deploying our website to a live server. Heroku is a Platform as a Service (PaaS) that can be used to host web applications in the cloud. It started as a Ruby-only service, but has expanded to support lots of different languages and frameworks. Deploying a Sinatra application on Heroku is straightforward and, best of all, free for basic sites!

To get started, head over to Heroku and sign up for an account.[2] Once you've done this, install the Heroku Toolbelt.[3] This provides you with the following software utilities: a command line interface that's used to communicate with Heroku; Foreman, which is used to run applications locally; and Git, a revision control system that is used to deploy sites to Heroku.

### Git in a Nutshell

Git is a distributed revision control system that was developed by Linus Torvalds, developer of the Linux kernel. It allows you to track changes in your code, make different branches of code, and "roll back" to previous versions. It's perfect for people working in teams, as every team member has their own repository that they can make changes to. These changes can then be merged with other members' repositories. It is an essential part of the workflow when deploying applications to Heroku, but is invaluable for keeping all projects under revision control. GitHub[4]

---

[1] This is when a malicious link from another site will try to exploit the fact that a user is still logged in to your application.

[2] https://api.heroku.com/signup

[3] https://toolbelt.heroku.com/

[4] https://github.com

is an online place to keep repositories and share code, and is well worth looking into for any developer. In fact, Sinatra itself is developed using Git and is also hosted on GitHub.

# Creating a Heroku App

Upon installing the Heroku Toolbelt, you should now have access to the `heroku` command from within the terminal. First of all, try logging in using the same details as when you signed up for Heroku.

To create a Heroku app, we use the command `heroku create` followed by the name of the app. In our case, we want to call the app `songs-by-sinatra`, so we'd use the following command:

```
$ heroku create songs-by-sinatra-from-daz
```

Unfortunately, you won't be able to use the name `songs-by-sinatra`, because I've already taken it! You can choose your own app name, or just leave it blank and Heroku will allocate a name for you.

# Bundler

Bundler is a program that helps manage all the gems used by an application. It is particularly useful at ensuring that the gems used are the same in development and production. Let's install the bundler gem to start:

```
$ gem install bundler
```

## Gemfile

Bundler uses a Gemfile to keep track of all the gems used by the application. Create an empty file and save it as **Gemfile** (no extension). Inside this file, list all the gems that our application uses, like so:

```
                                                        chapter04/Gemfile
source :rubygems
gem "sinatra"
gem "slim"
gem "sass"
```

```
gem "dm-core"
gem "dm-migrations"
gem "thin"
gem "pg", :group => :production
gem "dm-postgres-adapter", :group => :production
gem "dm-sqlite-adapter", :group => :development
```

You can specify a certain version or place some gems in groups. Here, we're using production and development groups to differentiate between the fact that we are using SQLite locally, while Heroku uses PostgreSQL.

Once the Gemfile has been created, we use Bundler to install all these gems, then lock them down to the versions being used with the following command:

```
$ bundle install --without production
```

This should create a new file called **Gemfile.lock** that contains all the gems we are using, as well as their dependencies. The `--without production` flag ensures that any gems that were placed in the production group aren't installed locally.

## Rack It Up!

Next, we create a rackup file, which are configuration files used by Rack apps. For our purposes, Heroku uses them to run Sinatra applications. We create a text file, save it as **config.ru**, and place the following code inside it:

chapter04/config.ru

```
require './main'
run Sinatra::Application
```

There's little to it, really; it just tells Rack the name of the file we're using, and then starts the Sinatra application running. It's also possible to put more settings and configuration into a rackup file, as we'll see later, but this will be fine for now.

## Git

To be able to deploy to Heroku, we'll need to place all our code in a Git repository.

We'll initialize an empty Git repository in our application directory by typing the following command:

```
$ git init
```

If you're yet to set up Git, it's worth establishing your username and email address (used to label the commits that you make) with the following commands:

```
$ git config user.name "DAZ"
$ git config user.email "example@sitepoint.com"
```

Next, we'll add all the current directory files to the repository using this command:

```
$ git add .
```

And last of all, we will commit these changes to the repository using the `commit` command. In addition, we'll attach a message that describes the changes that have just been made to the repository, using the `-m` flag:

```
$ git commit -m 'initial commit'
```

Now all our code is safely under version control.

 **Git Tutorials**

There are loads of free Git resources out there if you want to learn more about Git. Here are a few for starters:

**GitHub (https://help.github.com/)**
    has extremely useful help pages

**Git Magic (http://www-cs-students.stanford.edu/~blynn/gitmagic/)**
    uses some great metaphors to explain how Git works

**Git Immersion (http://gitimmersion.com/)**
    is beautifully presented and easy to follow in a step-by-step tutorial format

**Pro Git (http://git-scm.com/book)**
    is a full book available for free online

# Deploying to Heroku

Now we'll go ahead and create an app on Heroku by typing the following command in the terminal:

```
$ heroku create songs-by-sinatra-from-daz
```

Once this is done, deploying the website is a cinch. Run the following command:

```
$ git push heroku master
```

You should receive a message confirming that your application has been deployed to Heroku along the lines of:

```
-----> Launching... done, v4
       http://songs-by-sinatra-from-daz.herokuapp.com deployed to He
➥roku
```

Our website is now live on the Internet!

We can see it by typing the following command:

```
$ heroku open
```

This should open up a browser window showing our live website.

 **Troubleshooting Heroku**

> If you find your app is failing to deploy on Heroku, try using this command to see what's going wrong:
>
> ```
> $ heroku logs
> ```

# Setting up the Database on Heroku

Our website is functioning fine, except for the song pages that use a database back end. This is because we're yet to configure the database to run on Heroku's servers. Heroku uses a PostgreSQL database and a URL in an environment variable called

ENV['DATABASE_URL']. Move your :development database configuration from **song.rb** to **main.rb**, and ensure the correct database will be used in production like so:

```
                                          chapter04/main.rb (excerpt)
configure :development do
  DataMapper.setup(:default, "sqlite3://#{Dir.pwd}/development.db")
end

configure :production do
  DataMapper.setup(:default, ENV['DATABASE_URL'])
end
```

This specifies two separate databases for the different environments: SQLite in development on our local machine and PostgreSQL in production on Heroku.

Because we've just changed the code, we use Git to add the changes to our repository using the following commands:

```
$ git add .
```

Next, we commit these changes, with a message about what we did:

```
$ git commit -m 'added database configuration'
```

Last of all, we push the changes to Heroku:

```
$ git push heroku master
```

These changes become live immediately. It is a very common workflow when working with Git and Heroku: make changes, add, commit, push—and it will soon become second nature!

One last point to remember is to create the database on Heroku's servers, since the database we're using only exists locally. To do this, we need to use Heroku's console:

```
$ heroku run console
```

This works just like an IRB session. We require our **main.rb** file and run the same command we used in the section called "Migrations" in Chapter 3 to create the database table:

```
> require './main'
```

```
> DataMapper.auto_migrate!
```

Now if you go to the live website at http://*yourappname*.herokuapp.com/songs, everything should be working as it does on our local version.

# Time to Shine

In this chapter, we covered how to configure Sinatra using configure blocks. We also explored how you can use a different configure block for each environment: development, test, and production. Next, we looked at settings, including some of Sinatra's built-in settings, and saw how to make your own customized ones.

We introduced sessions and employed them to build a simple login system for our Songs By Sinatra website. Then we used Heroku to deploy the site live to the Web. Along the way, we installed and used the Git revision control system.

In the next chapter, we'll be introducing helper methods and looking at how to use them to make development easier. We'll also address using external gems to add extra functionality to an application.

# Helpers and Finders

In the last chapter, we identified how to configure settings in Sinatra in different environments and finished by deploying our site live on the Heroku platform. In this chapter, we'll learn about using helper methods to make our code easier to read and less repetitive.

We'll also look at using external gems to add extra functionality to our application. In particular, we'll use the Sinatra::Flash gem to provide feedback messages after redirects, and the Pony gem to help send an email from our application's contact page.

To finish off, we'll build our own extension that uses the login functionality from the previous chapter to protect certain pages of our application.

## Helper Methods

**Helper methods** (or helpers, for short) are snippets of code that can be repeatedly used in route handlers and views. If a piece of code is long and complicated, it makes sense to wrap it up in a helper method so that the route handlers don't fill up with hard-to-follow code.

Helper methods make an application's code easier to read and follow. They're particularly useful to DRY up the code if there are tasks that often need carrying out.

There are loads of helpers already built into Sinatra, but we can also write our own helper methods … which is exactly what we're going to do in this chapter!

# Helpers Block

Creating helper methods is easy; they're just ordinary methods that are placed inside a `helpers` block like so:

```
helpers do
  # helper methods go here
end
```

Any methods defined in this block can be used within route handlers or views too. To demonstrate, let's build a couple of simple helpers to improve our application.

## Linking to Stylesheets

First, let's create a helper method for adding stylesheet `link` tags to our application. Currently, we have one stylesheet `link` tag that's hardcoded into our layout file:

*chapter05/views/layout.slim (excerpt)*

```
link rel="stylesheet" href="/styles.css"
```

At some point, we may want to add more stylesheets to our application, so let's make a helper method that makes this task easier. Open up **main.rb** and add the following `helpers` block after the configuration block:

*chapter05/main.rb (excerpt)*

```
helpers do
  def css(*stylesheets)
    stylesheets.map do |stylesheet|
      "<link href=\"/#{stylesheet}.css\" media=\"screen, projection\
➡" rel=\"stylesheet\" />"
    end.join
  end
end
```

This creates a helper method called `css` that accepts any number arguments (signified by the `*` before the `stylesheets` argument). A stylesheet `link` tag is then generated for each argument. The arguments are the filenames of the stylesheet (without the .css extension), and can be given as strings or symbols. For example, this code:

```
== css :styles, :custom, :widgets
```

generates the following links:

```
<link href="/styles.css" media="screen projection"
  rel="stylesheet"/>
<link href="/custom.css" media="screen projection"
  rel="stylesheet"/>
<link href="/widgets.css" media="screen projection"
  rel="stylesheet"/>
```

Since we only have the one stylesheet (called **styles.css**) for now, we just replace the `link` tag in our **layout.slim** file with our new helper syntax:

chapter05/views/layout.slim *(excerpt)*

```
head
  title== @title || "Songs By Sinatra"
  meta charset="utf-8"
  == css :styles
```

While it only saves us a small amount of work at this stage, it does save us from having to remember the `link` tag notation, and will make it easier if we want to add more stylesheets in the future.

## Styling the Current Page

The next helper method will check to see if the `href` attribute of a link on a page is the same as the current path that was requested by the user; in other words, does the link point to the page to which we've just navigated? We can obtain this information using a method of Rack's `request` object called `path`: `request.path`.

This will return the path of the page that's currently being visited, relative to the root URL—the same type of paths that we use in our route handlers. We're going to create a helper method called `current?` that will add a class of `current` to any links that point to the page presently being viewed. This class will enable us to style them differently from other links to show the user they're already on that page. Here's the code that needs to be put inside the `helpers` block:

chapter05/main.rb *(excerpt)*

```ruby
helpers do
  def css(*stylesheets)
    stylesheets.map do |stylesheet|
      "<link href=\"/#{stylesheet}.css\" media=\"screen, projection\
➥" rel=\"stylesheet\" />"
    end.join
  end

  def current?(path='/')
    (request.path==path || request.path==path+'/') ? "current" : nil
  end
end
```

This uses Ruby's ternary operator, `?`, to check if the path supplied as an argument to the helper is the same as the current path given by `request.path`. (Note, some setups result in `request.path` receiving a trailing slash, so we need to plan for both outcomes.) If they're the same, we simply return the string `"current"`. If not, a value of `nil` is returned. To use this helper, we employ it in views when specifying the `class` attribute of links. In fact, a good place to use this is in the `nav` element in our layout file. Change the code in the `nav` block so that it looks like the following:

chapter05/views/nav.slim

```slim
nav
  ul
    li
      a href=="/" title="Home" class==current? Home
    li
      a href=="/about" class==current?("/about") title="About" About
    li
      a href=="/contact" class==current?("/contact") title="Contact"
➥ Contact
    li
      a href=="/songs" class==current?("/songs") title="Songs" Songs
```

Now these links will have a class of `current` if they link to the page that's currently being shown. And if they're not linking to the current page, there will be no `class` attribute at all (because `nil` was returned from the `current?` method).

All we have to do now is add a slightly different style for links that are for the current page. Let's use a Sass function called `lighten` to make them five percent lighter than the other links by adding the following to **styles.scss**:

chapter05/views/styles.scss *(excerpt)*

```
nav a.current {
  background: lighten($black, 5%);
}
```

If you restart the server and look at any of the pages, you'll see that the tab for the current page is slightly lighter, as in Figure 5.1.

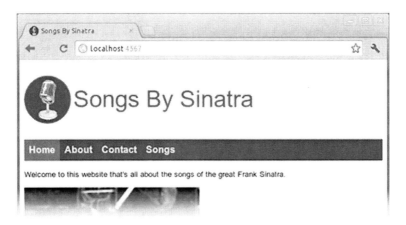

Figure 5.1. A lighter style

## Setting Titles

We'll now create a helper method to set the `title` element. Page titles can currently be set using the instance variable `@title` in the route handler. The `title` tag in the layout uses this, or falls back onto the name, "Songs By Sinatra":

chapter05/views/layout.slim *(excerpt)*

```
title== @title || "Songs By Sinatra"
```

Let's use a helper method to deal with setting the title in the main application, rather than in the layout. This can be done with a one-line helper method in the helpers block:

*chapter05/main.rb (excerpt)*

```ruby
def set_title
  @title ||= "Songs By Sinatra"
end
```

This method uses Ruby's conditional assignment operator, ||=, which will leave @title as if it has already been set; otherwise, it will be set to "Songs By Sinatra". Now, the title tag in our layout file just needs to be:

*chapter05/views/layout.slim (excerpt)*

```
title== @title
```

This helper needs to be applied to all our routes to set the title. Rather than doing this manually, we can simply call the method in a before filter. Anything inside a **before filter** block will be run before each request. To ensure that every page has a title set, we can add the following code to **main.rb** (it can go anywhere, but it is common to put it near the top of the file, after the settings and configuration):

*chapter05/main.rb (excerpt)*

```ruby
before do
  set_title
end
```

It might not be a surprise to learn that there's also an **after filter** that runs any code inside its block after every request.

 ## Pattern Matching in Routes

You can add a pattern as an argument to filters so that they only happen if the route matches that pattern. For example, the following filter will apply exclusively to any routes that start with /special/:

```ruby
after '/special/*' do
  # do something special
end
```

# Song Helpers Module

Next, we're going to create some helpers to make the route handlers in our song file read more nicely. But instead of placing the methods in the helpers block, we will create a module called `SongHelpers` to put them in. Open up **song.rb** and place the following code near the top of the file (after the `Song` class):

*chapter05/song.rb (excerpt)*

```ruby
module SongHelpers
  def find_songs
    @songs = Song.all
  end

  def find_song
    Song.get(params[:id])
  end

  def create_song
    @song = Song.create(params[:song])
  end
end
```

Here we have three fairly straightforward methods for the `Song` class: the first is `find_songs`, which simply fetches all the songs (though this could be modified in future to accept an argument to give a more selective search). The second method, `find_song` (note this is singular), finds a particular song in the database using the value of `params[:id]`. The last method, `create_song` method instantiates a new Song object using the attributes in the `params[:song]` hash.

Next, we register these methods as helper methods. Place the following line after the module:

*chapter05/song.rb (excerpt)*

```ruby
  ⋮
  def create_song
    @song = Song.create(params[:song])
  end
end

helpers SongHelpers
```

Now we can use these methods in our route handlers. Change the following five route handlers so that they look like this:

chapter05/song.rb *(excerpt)*

```ruby
get '/songs' do
  find_songs
  slim :songs
end

get '/songs/new' do
  halt(401,'Not Authorized') unless session[:admin]
  @song = Song.new
  slim :new_song
end

get '/songs/:id' do
  @song = find_song
  slim :show_song
end

get '/songs/:id/edit' do
  @song = find_song
  slim :edit_song
end

post '/songs' do
  create_song
  redirect to("/songs/#{@song.id}")
end

put '/songs/:id' do
  song = find_song
  song.update(params[:song])
  redirect to("/songs/#{song.id}")
end

delete '/songs/:id' do
  find_song.destroy
  redirect to('/songs')
end
```

While no functionality has been added with these helpers, the code in the route handlers is now much more readable. Refactoring code such as this is an important step when building applications, as it makes the code easier to maintain. You should always be on the lookout for ways to make your route handlers leaner by abstracting code into reusable helpers.

# External Gems

There are a number of Sinatra extensions that add extra functionality to Sinatra and are available as gems. We're going to look at a couple of them in this chapter to help improve the functionality of our application.

## Sinatra::Flash

Sinatra::Flash[1] is an extension that lets you store information between requests. Often, when an application processes a request, it will redirect to another URL upon finishing, which generates another request. This means that any information from the previous request is lost (due to the stateless nature of HTTP). Sinatra::Flash overcomes this by providing access to *the flash*—a hash-like object that stores temporary values such as error messages so that they can be retrieved later—usually on the next request. It also removes the information once it's been used. All this can be achieved via sessions (and that's exactly how Sinatra::Flash does it), but Sinatra::Flash is easy to implement and provides a number of helper methods.

 **Frugal Flash**

Sinatra::Flash copies all of its functionality from the flash found in Ruby on Rails; however, like most things in Sinatra, it uses much less code!

First, we install the `sinatra-flash` gem, like so:

```
$ gem install sinatra-flash
```

Add the `require 'sinatra/flash'` statement to the top of your **main.rb** file. Now we can place messages in the flash notice in our route handlers. One place where this is useful is in our **song.rb** file. Open it up and edit the following POST route handler so that it looks like the code that follows:

---

[1] https://github.com/SFEley/sinatra-flash

```
                                              chapter05/song.rb (excerpt)
post '/songs' do
  flash[:notice] = "Song successfully added" if create_song
  redirect to("/songs/#{@song.id}")
end
```

This appends a message to the flash confirming that the song has been successfully added to the database; then it redirects to the next page. The message has a key of :notice, but you can use any key that you like. To test this out, we put the flash into our views. Sinatra::Flash provides a useful helper method called styled-flash that creates some HTML if the flash has any entries. The best place to put this helper is in our layout file. Place the following line on the line above == yield in layout.slim:

```
                                     chapter05/views/layout.slim (excerpt)
section
  == styled_flash
```

Try adding a song and then checking the HTML created after the redirect to the song page. It should contain the following:

```
<div id='flash'>
  <div class='flash notice'>
    Song successfully added
  <div>
</div>
```

This gives us some hooks that we can use for styling the flash. To start off, add the following to styles.scss to place the message in a pink box:

```
                                     chapter05/views/styles.scss (excerpt)
.flash {
  width: 600px;
  padding: 5px;
  font-weight: bold;
  margin: 20px;
  background: lighten($red, 60%);
```

```
    color: $red;
    border: 1px solid $red;
}
```

Notice that we're using the $red variable that we created in the section called "Getting Sassy" in Chapter 2, along with the lighten function to ensure that the colors are consistent across the application? Now the flash is working, we can add it to the other route handlers that use redirect. Observe that in each case we only display the flash message conditionally based on the operation being successful:

chapter05/song.rb *(excerpt)*

```
put '/songs/:id' do
  protected!
  song = find_song
  if song.update(params[:song])
    flash[:notice] = "Song successfully updated"
  end
  redirect to("/songs/#{song.id}")
end

delete '/songs/:id' do
  if find_song.destroy
    flash[:notice] = "Song deleted"
  end
  redirect to('/songs')
end
```

 **Failing Gracefully**

We've taken care to display flash messages when the operations are successful only; our route handlers failed to cover the outcome when it's unfavorable. Therefore, it's a useful exercise to have a go at making the application fail a bit more gracefully.

Once this is saved, restart the server and have a go at creating, updating, and deleting some songs. You should see a similar sight to Figure 5.2.

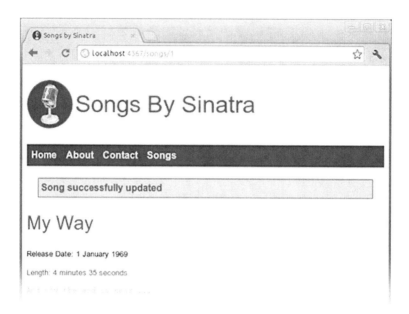

Figure 5.2. Certainly no flash in the pan

## Pony Mail

It's fair to say that our Contact page is a bit basic at the moment, with just an email
address people can use. It's relatively easy to create a contact form, which generates
an email that's then sent to us. Sinatra has no email functionality baked in, but this
can be easily provided by the Pony gem.[2] Install it using the following code:

```
$ gem install pony
```

Remember to add `require 'pony'` to your **main.rb** file as usual. Now we'll add a
form to the Contact page. Open up **contact.slim** and change it to this:

chapter05/views/contact.slim

```
p You can contact me by filling in the form below:
form action="/contact" method="POST"
  label for="name" Name:
  input type="text" name="name"
  label for="email" Email:
```

---

[2] http://rubygems.org/gems/pony

```
input type="text" name="email"
label for="message" Your Message:
textarea name="message"
input type="submit" value="Send Message"
```

This straightforward form contains fields for a name, an email address, and a short message. If you reached http://localhost:4567/contact, you should see something along the lines of Figure 5.3.

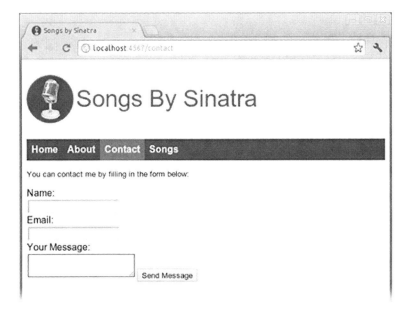

Figure 5.3. Fielding enquiries

Now we process the message and send it as an email when the form is submitted. The `action` and `method` attributes of the `form` tag tell us that the information is sent to the route `/contact` as a post request, so we can create a route handler to deal with it:

chapter05/main.rb *(excerpt)*

```
post '/contact' do
  send_message
  flash[:notice] = "Thank you for your message. We'll be in touch s
➥oon."
  redirect to('/')
end
```

This uses the helper method `send_message` to deal with the message that was posted. We're yet to actually create this helper method, but it fits in with our new mantra of keeping our route handlers short and descriptive (and there's quite a lot of code for dealing with the message, so this definitely make sense). We're also using the flash to display a thank-you message to the user before redirecting them back to the Home page. Let's now create that helper method—the following method goes in the `helpers` block:

*chapter05/main.rb (excerpt)*

```ruby
def send_message
  Pony.mail(
    :from => params[:name] + "<" + params[:email] + ">",
    :to => 'daz@gmail.com',
    :subject => params[:name] + " has contacted you",
    :body => params[:message],
    :port => '587',
    :via => :smtp,
    :via_options => {
      :address            => 'smtp.gmail.com',
      :port               => '587',
      :enable_starttls_auto => true,
      :user_name          => 'daz',
      :password           => 'secret',
      :authentication     => :plain,
      :domain             => 'localhost.localdomain'
    })
end
```

As you can see, there's quite a lot of code there. Most of it is a mixture of standard options for Pony and you can just copy them straight down, but the following will need changing for your application:

**:to =>**      This needs to be your own email address.

**:address =>**   If you don't have a Gmail account, you should change this to your mail provider's address.

**:username =>**  This is the username with which you access your email.

**:password =>**  This is the password you use to access your email account.

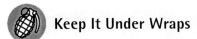

## Keep It Under Wraps

Be careful not to make any of your code public if it contains any of this information!

Give this a test. Fill in the form, press send, and you should receive an email from your application! Cool, huh?

## Email in Production

For email to work in our production environment, we'll use a Heroku add-on called SendGrid.[3] This lets you send up to 200 emails a day from your application for free. Paid-for plans are also available if you need to send more. To install this add-on, type the following code into a command prompt:

```
$ heroku addons:add sendgrid:starter
```

For it to work, we'll make a few changes to our code. The best way to do this is to edit our `send_message` helper so that it receives the correct settings. We will then place the different configuration settings in the relevant configure blocks:

*chapter05/main.rb (excerpt)*

```
configure :development do
  DataMapper.setup(:default, "sqlite3://#{Dir.pwd}/development.db")
  set :email_address => 'smtp.gmail.com',
      :email_user_name => 'daz',
      :email_password => 'secret',
      :email_domain => 'localhost.localdomain'
end

configure :production do
  DataMapper.setup(:default, ENV['DATABASE_URL'])
  set :email_address => 'smtp.sendgrid.net',
      :email_user_name => ENV['SENDGRID_USERNAME'],
      :email_password => ENV['SENDGRID_PASSWORD'],
      :email_domain => 'heroku.com'
end
```

---

[3] http://sendgrid.com/

This keeps the settings we employed for the development environment and uses the required settings for SendGrid in the production environment. Notice that we only need to use the `set` method once if we enter the multiple settings as a hash.

`ENV['SENDGRID_USERNAME']` and `ENV['SENDGRID_PASSWORD']` are Heroku environment variables; they are values that are kept securely on Heroku's servers and are created automatically when you install the SendGrid add-on. If you want to see all the environment variables that are set on your application that Heroku uses, try the following command:

```
$ heroku config
```

You can also add your own using the following command:

```
$ heroku config:add NAME=Frank
```

Now that we've configured our email contact form to work on Heroku, we'll add the following lines to our Gemfile so that the new gems are included:

chapter05/Gemfile *(excerpt)*

```
gem "sinatra-flash"
gem "pony"
```

Last of all, we run the following commands to bundle the new gems and then push all the changes to our live server. As usual, we'll use the following commands:

```
$ bundle install --without production
```

```
$ git add .
```

```
$ git commit -m 'Added email contact form'
```

```
$ git push heroku master
```

Now your live site includes a nice contact form. Why not use it to send yourself a congratulatory email?

# Sinatra::Contrib

We've just used two external gems to add some extra functionality to our application. The Sinatra::Contrib project[4] aims to collect lots of useful functionality into one gem, with different modules that can be used as required. We have already seen the really useful `sinatra-reloader` in the section called "Your First Sinatra App" in Chapter 1. Other extensions include:

`sinatra-cookies`
> provides helpers for reading and writing cookies more easily

`sinatra-respond_with`
> allows you to process a request based on the MIME type requested in the header

`sinatra-content_for`
> provides a `content_for` helper that works the same as the one found in Ruby on Rails; basically, it allows you to insert custom blocks of view code into pre-defined content blocks in the layout

`sinatra-namespace`
> provides namespace support, allowing you to define parts of the application that only apply to certain namespaces

`sinatra-json`
> adds a JSON helper method that allows you to generate and return JSON documents

`sinatra-test_helpers`
> provides a number of methods to help make testing easier

It's well worth installing the `sinatra-contrib` gem (`gem install sinatra-contrib`) and having a play around with some of these extensions, especially if you feel your application needs a bit of extra functionality.

---

[4] https://github.com/sinatra/sinatra-contrib

## Admin Extension

In Chapter 4, we used sessions to create route handlers that allowed users to log in and out of the application. You can remove that code from **song.rb** and **main.rb**, because we're now going to create some useful helper methods that protect pages and check whether a user is logged in or not. We're also going to register helper methods another way—as a Sinatra extension. Extensions go in separate files and include helper methods, settings, and route handlers. To use the extension, you require the file in your application. This makes them reusable, and they can also be packaged as a gem for distribution. To produce the extension, create a new folder in the root directory called **sinatra**. Inside this folder, create a new file called **auth.rb**. The full code for this extension is shown:

```
chapter05/sinatra/auth.rb

require 'sinatra/base'  (1)
require 'sinatra/flash'  (2)

module Sinatra
  module Auth  (3)
    module Helpers  (4)
      def authorized?  (5)
        session[:admin]
      end

      def protected!  (6)
        halt 401,slim(:unauthorized) unless authorized?  (7)
      end
    end

    def self.registered(app)  (8)
      app.helpers Helpers  (9)

      app.enable :sessions  (10)

      app.set :username => 'frank',  (11)
              :password => 'sinatra'

      app.get '/login' do  (12)
        slim :login
      end

      app.post '/login' do
```

```
        if params[:username] == settings.username && params[:passwo
➥rd] == settings.password
          session[:admin] = true
          flash[:notice] = "You are now logged in as #{settings.use
➥rname}"
          redirect to('/songs')
        else
          flash[:notice] = "The username or password you entered ar
➥e incorrect"
          redirect to('/login')
        end
      end

      app.get '/logout' do
        session[:admin] = nil
        flash[:notice] = "You have now logged out"
        redirect to('/')
      end
    end
  end
  register Auth ⑬
end
```

❶  At the top of the file, we require 'sinatra/base'. Every Sinatra extension has
    to require this file—it is the core of Sinatra minus the code needed to be an
    actual application.

❷  We're also requiring Sinatra::Flash as the extension will use flash for displaying
    messages after the user logs in and out.

❸  Our extension is then created as a module nested inside a Sinatra module.
    This is the standard structure for all Sinatra extensions.

❹  We place the helper methods that our extension will use at the start of the
    module. These are created inside their own module called Helpers (you can
    call it whatever you like, but Helpers seems to make sense).

❺  Inside the Helpers module, we've added two helper methods. The first is
    authorized?, which checks to see if a user has logged in by checking if the
    value of session[:admin] is true. This is a good method to use in route
    handlers and views.

⑥   The second method is `protected!`. It specifies that a route handler can only be accessed by a user who is logged in (notice that it utilizes the `authorized?` helper method to check this).

⑦   This uses Sinatra's `halt` method, which immediately stops a request and returns a specified HTTP code (401 in this case). It also shows a view called `unauthorized`, which we'll produce shortly and save in our **views** directory.

⑧   After the helpers, we'll devise a method called `self.registered(app)`. This contains all the settings for the extension, and all the route handlers. It also specifies the name of the helpers module that we just created. Inside this, all the methods need to be methods of the **app** object, which is the argument passed to `self.registered`, and is, in fact, the application using the extension.

### Gem of an Extension

If you have installed the Sinatra::Contrib gem, it has a handy module called `sinatra-extension` that lets you write extensions without having to add settings, configuration, and route handlers as methods of the application. To use it, you need to require it at the top of the extension file and then include it in the extension module. If we were to use it in our **Auth** extension, the start of the file would look like this:

```
require 'sinatra/extension'
Module Sinatra
  extend Sinatra::Extension
```

Now instead of **app.get** `'/login'`, we can simply write `get` `'/login'`.

⑨   This line says to use the module called `Helpers` for the helpers.

⑩   After this, we enable `sessions` …

⑪   … and create some settings. These settings can be overridden in **main.rb**, which means that you can change all the settings used by the extension without having to touch the extension file. They are just default settings.

⑫   Then there are the route handlers. These are much the same as those that we created in the last chapter, although we're now using Sinatra::Flash to add some nice messages when the user logs in and out.

⓭ Finally, at the end of the file, we register the extension.

Once you've saved the file, add this line to the list of requires at the top of **main.rb**:

*chapter05/main.rb (excerpt)*

```
require './sinatra/auth'
```

Finally, as mentioned in point ❼, we need an `unauthorized` view:

*chapter05/views/unauthorized.slim*

```
h1 Unauthorized
p You need to be <a href="/login">logged in</a> to view this page.
```

Restart the server, and you should be able to log in and out using our new extension. To make it easier for our users, let's add a link so that they can do this in a footer. We want this to be on every page, so let's add the following code to the bottom of **layout.slim** within the body:

*chapter05/views/layout.slim (excerpt)*

```
footer
  - if authorized?
    a href="/logout" log out
  - else
    a href="/login" log in
```

This uses the `authorized?` helper to check if the user is logged in or not, and then presents the relevant link (to either log in or out).

Our last task is to utilize the `protected!` method to require users to log in to certain pages. For example, the page for creating a new song should only be available to a user who is logged in, so it should have the `protected!` method placed at the start of the route handler. Open up **song.rb** and change it so that it looks like the following:

*chapter05/song.rb (excerpt)*

```
get '/songs/new' do
  protected!
```

I'd strongly advise you to add the `protected!` method to the create, edit, update, and delete route handlers too!

### Changing the Username and Password

The point of making the `Auth` extension is so that it can be reused in other applications, but it's highly unlikely that other applications will want to use the same username and password (not to mention the security risk). Changing these is straightforward, though; instead of editing the **auth.rb** file, you can just set them from within **main.rb**, like so:

```
set :username, 'daz'
set :password, 'secret'
```

Settings in the main application file will always supersede the default settings in the extension file, making it easy to customize an extension's settings without having to go poking around in the extension's code.

# A Little Help from My Friends

In this chapter, we introduced the concept of helper methods for keeping our code tidy and reusable. We created some helpers that could be used in the views to make them read better, and added some functionality for styling current pages. We also created some helper methods that removed any complicated logic out of the route handlers and made them easier to read.

After this, we used the Sinatra::Flash and Pony gems to add extra functionality to our application. We also installed the SendGrid add-on on Heroku to allow us to send email on our production server. We finished off by creating our own Sinatra extension that allows users to log in and out of our application. This provided a couple of handy helper methods that allowed us to check if a user was logged in, and ensured that a route required a user to be logged in before it could be accessed.

In the next chapter, we will look at how we can use JavaScript in our application, including utilizing CoffeeScript to make writing JavaScript more enjoyable. We'll also be using jQuery to help process requests asynchronously.

# Jazzing up with JavaScript

Our web application is now coming along nicely—we have a number of pages, a database of songs, login functionality, and an email contact form. In this chapter we're going to go use JavaScript to add some extra effects and functionality to the front end of the application.

We won't be getting our hands dirty writing JavaScript, though. Instead, we'll use CoffeeScript—a nicer alternative to all the brackets and curly braces of JavaScript —that will then be compiled into JavaScript for us.

In addition, we'll be using the jQuery library to add a date-picker to the song form to make entering a date easier. Then we'll finish off by adding a **Like** button to each song, so that users can show their love for the song. This will utilize Ajax to communicate with the server in the background.

## CoffeeScript

CoffeeScript[1] is a language that compiles into JavaScript. It was written by Jeremy Ashkenas in 2009 as an attempt to make writing JavaScript a smoother experience.

---

[1] http://coffeescript.org/

The syntax is more Ruby-like, and it helps to streamline JavaScript into shorter, easier-to-read code that is more maintainable. It has become very popular over the last few years, particularly in the Ruby community, and has been incorporated into Ruby on Rails from version 3.1.

We're going to use CoffeeScript to produce the JavaScript used by our application in the rest of the book because of the benefits I've just cited. Writing CoffeeScript can take some getting used to at first, though, especially if you've written JavaScript. Luckily, the website has a great interactive tutorial that will take you through the syntax's basics. If you want to learn more about CoffeeScript, you could also take a look at *Jump Start CoffeeScript* by Earle Castledine.[2]

## CoffeeScript in Sinatra

Using CoffeeScript in Sinatra is a piece of cake. To get started, we install a couple of gems: `coffee-script`, which compiles the CoffeeScript, and `therubyracer`, which embeds the V8 JavaScript engine into Ruby, allowing it to interpret JavaScript:

```
$ gem install coffee-script therubyracer
```

 **Node.js Has Your Back**

Installing The Ruby Racer gem is unnecessary if you have Node.js installed on your system. You will, however, still need it to run on Heroku.

Now we require the V8 engine and CoffeeScript in our application by adding this line to the top of **main.rb**:

chapter06/main.rb *(excerpt)*

```
require 'v8'
require 'coffee-script'
```

Good practice dictates that we put our JavaScript in a separate file. This needs a link in **layout.slim**, which we'll add just below the stylesheet link:

---

[2] http://www.sitepoint.com/books/coffeescript1/

```
== css :styles
script src="/javascripts/application.js"
```

The JavaScript file referred to in the src attribute doesn't actually exist (we're yet to even have a **javascripts** folder in the public directory!). As mentioned, we're going to create our JavaScript file using CoffeeScript, which will be in a file in the **views** directory. To ensure Sinatra deals with this, we add the following route handler in **main.rb**:

```
get('/styles.css'){ scss :styles }
get('/javascripts/application.js'){ coffee :application }
```

This employs the `coffee` helper method to tell Sinatra to process the request using CoffeeScript. It utilizes a CoffeeScript file called **application** in the **views** directory. Let's create that file now, save it as **application.coffee** in the **views** directory, and place the following code inside:

```
alert 'Hello!'
```

This is a basic example to test that all is working. Save it, start the server running, and visit any page on our web application. If it's working as it should be, all the pages on the local site should now have a popup saying "Hello!" as in Figure 6.1.

Figure 6.1. The Hello! alert: a reassuring sign

What's happening is that the CoffeeScript is being compiled into JavaScript on the server. You can see the compiled JavaScript that is output by visiting http://localhost:4567/javascripts/application.js, which should look like this:

```
(function() {
  alert('Hello!');
}).call(this);
```

As you can see in this code, the JavaScript produced by CoffeeScript follows the best practice of wrapping all the JavaScript in a self-executing function. This avoids any clashes with other JavaScript files in the global scope.

Now we know that we can create JavaScript using CoffeeScript, we can go on and add some nice effects to our application. But rather than write all this from scratch, we'll use the incredibly useful jQuery library.

## jQuery

jQuery[3] is a popular JavaScript library that makes navigating a document easier. It also includes some basic effects and Ajax functionality. It was written in 2006 by John Resig, and quickly gained popularity. This open-source project is now maintained by the jQuery Team and actively developed by a vibrant community.

---

[3] http://jquery.com/

There are a number of effects in the jQuery UI library[4] with literally hundreds of third-party plugins that add extra functionality to the front end of applications. If you want to really master jQuery, I can recommend reading *JQuery: Novice to Ninja* by Earle Castledine and Craig Sharkie.[5]

To use jQuery and the jQuery UI, we include a link to the JavaScript files in our HTML pages. The jQuery UI also needs a stylesheet styling the UI elements (such as sliders and calendar widgets). These are just plain old JavaScript files that can be downloaded from the jQuery website, but you can also link to the files on the jQuery Content Delivery Network (CDN), which means we avoid having to keep the files on our own server.

The following code includes the latest versions of jQuery and the jQuery UI, as well as the UI stylesheet, and should go above the link to the **application.js** in **layout.slim**:

*chapter06/views/layout.slim (excerpt)*

```
link href="http://code.jquery.com/ui/1.9.1/themes/base/jquery-ui.css
➥" media="screen, projection" rel="stylesheet"
script src="http://code.jquery.com/jquery-1.8.2.min.js"
script src="http://code.jquery.com/ui/1.9.0/jquery-ui.js"
script src="/javascripts/application.js"
```

Visit the jQuery website to find the latest version of these libraries, rather than use the version specified here. You can also customize your UI library so that it only has the modules you require, leading to less JavaScript to download.

### Content Delivery Networks

A Content Delivery Network (CDN) is a distributed system of web servers that aim to deliver content to users quickly and efficiently. A large number of CDNs are available for JavaScript libraries. The idea is that if lots of sites use the same CDN or "hotlink," it will be cached locally on the user's machine, saving the user from an extra download across all those sites. The downside is a loss of control and the chance (however small) that the CDN might go down and be unavailable.

---

[4] http://jqueryui.com/
[5] http://www.sitepoint.com/books/jquery2

There are pros and cons of using this method, discussed in this informative post by Craig Buckler.[6]

If you'd prefer to ignore jQuery CDNs, just download the files and save them in the public directory of your application.

# Date Picker

jQuery UI has a nifty date picker widget that displays a calendar for users to pick a date; it saves them from having to type it in directly, which can be awkward. It is also easy to implement once we have the relevant JavaScript included. In fact, it's just a few lines in **application.coffee**:

```
chapter06/views/application.coffee (excerpt)

$ ->
  $('#released_on')
  .datepicker( changeYear: true, yearRange: '1940:2000' )
```

This starts with the ubiquitous jQuery $ function that all of your jQuery code should be wrapped in. The next line finds the date `input` field because it has the `id` of `released_on` (jQuery uses CSS selector syntax to find elements on a web page, so in this case it is `#released_on`). It then uses the `datepicker()` method to add the relevant functionality. We have also specified some options as a JavaScript object literal that allow the year to be changed (`changeYear: true`) and limit the years to go from 1940 to 2000 (`yearRange: '1940:2000'`), which is roughly the time span that Sinatra's songs were published. All the options for the date picker widget can be found on the jQuery UI documentation page.[7]

Now have a go at creating or updating a song, and you should see a similar sight to Figure 6.2 when you click in the date `input` field.

---

[6] http://www.sitepoint.com/should-you-use-a-cdn/
[7] http://api.jqueryui.com/datepicker/

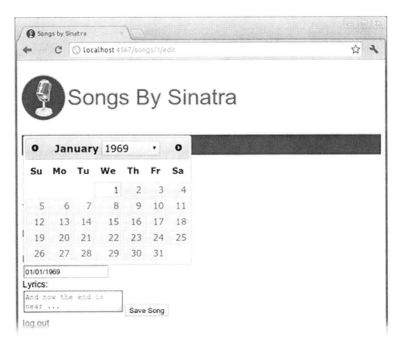

Figure 6.2. A date to remember

Before we move on, let's commit these changes to our Git repository:

```
$ git add .
$ git commit -m 'Added CoffeeScript and jQuery and implemented a ca
➥lendar widget'
```

# Adding a Like Button

Let's now add some more functionality to our application. We're going to follow in the footsteps of popular social media sites and add a **like** button to each song. This enables users to click on the button if they like a song, and will keep track of how many times it has been "liked."

## Git Branches

Since we're adding a new feature and now using Git to manage our code, we should take advantage of its ability to branch our code. Git keeps different branches of your code; you can see them by typing the following into a command prompt when in the root directory of your application:

```
$ git branch
* master
```

You should see that there's only one branch—the default branch—called "master." The asterisk (*) next to it indicates that it's the branch currently being used.

Whenever you decide to add a new feature to your application, it's a good idea to branch the code. This way, the master branch is protected if everything goes wrong. Once the branch is working correctly, you can merge the changes back into the master branch. To add a new branch called "like," enter the following command:

```
$ git branch like
```

Then check that it's been created:

```
$ git branch
  like
* master
```

The new branch has been created, but we're still on the master branch. To change to the "like" branch, use the `checkout` command:

```
$ git checkout like
Switched to branch 'like'
```

Now we can make changes without worrying about wrecking the master branch!

## Like Button

Before we implement the **Like** button, we'll add a new property to our Song class that keeps track of how many times a song has been liked. We'll call this `likes` and make it an `Integer` (you can't have half a like!) Adding an extra property using DataMapper is easy—we just open up **song.rb** and add the following property to the Song class:

chapter06/song.rb *(excerpt)*

```
property :likes, Integer, :default => 0
```

Notice that we've provided a default value of zero. This is because all songs start with zero likes; without this as a default value, the initial value would be nil, and that may cause problems when we want to query how many times a song has been "liked" and it's yet to have any likes.

 **Nil Is Not Zero!**

> `nil` is a special object in Ruby; it's actually one of only two objects that have a Boolean value of `false` (the other being `false` itself). This means that it is different to the number zero, `0`, or an empty string, `" "`.

We now update the database table with this new property. To do this, we go into IRB and require the **main.rb** file:

```
$ irb
irb> require './main'
=> true
```

Now we just use DataMapper's brilliant `auto_upgrade!` method, which updates our database table without destroying any of the data that's already there:

```
irb> DataMapper.auto_upgrade!
```

It's easy to underestimate the awesomeness of this method if you haven't worked with other database interfaces before. Changing the table structure mid-project would normally result in a world of pain making the database work. This method allows us to iterate rapidly while building the application, adding new features and properties as and when needed.

Let's just check that it worked. Stay in IRB and try the following query:

```
irb> song = Song.first
irb> song.likes
=> 0
```

This verifies that the first song that was already saved in the database now has a `likes` property, and is set to the default value of zero. Now we can move on and implement the **Like** button on each song's page.

Open up **show_song.slim** in the **views** directory and add the following code after the song lyrics:

```
                                    chapter06/views/show_song.slim (excerpt)
pre= @song.lyrics
#like ❶
  == slim :like ❷
  form action="/songs/#{@song.id}/like" method="POST" ❸
    input type="submit" value="Like" ❹
```

❶ This creates a div element with an id of like (which will be a useful hook to refer to this element with JavaScript later).

❷ We're using a partial here called like, which displays a message indicating how many times the song has been "liked." This goes in its own view file as it contains quite a bit of logic; it will also be used when we add Ajax later.

❸ Our #like div contains a form with an action attribute, which posts the form to a URL; for example, /songs/2/like.

❹ Finally, our form contains just one input button to press.

Save the following code as **like.slim** in the **views** folder:

```
                                              chapter06/views/like.slim
- if @song.likes == 0
  p Nobody has liked this song so far!
- if @song.likes == 1
  p This song has been liked once
- if @song.likes > 1
  p This song has been liked #{@song.likes} times
```

We'll create a route handler to deal with the POST URL. Add the following code to the bottom of **song.rb**:

```
                                              chapter06/song.rb (excerpt)
post '/songs/:id/like' do
  @song = find_song
  @song.likes = @song.likes.next
```

```
  @song.save
  redirect back
end
```

I hope this code is self-explanatory. It uses one of our song helpers from the previous chapter to find the song given in the URL, and assigns it to the variable @song. It then increases the number of "likes" by one using the next method, and saves it to the database. After this, we use the back helper method to redirect to the previous page that was requested, which, in this case, just reloads the same page. This has the effect of updating the **like.slim** partial with the new number of "likes."

Before we start "liking" some songs, let's add some style to make our button more attractive. Using the **like.png** I've supplied in the public folder, add the following code to the bottom of **styles.scss**:

*chapter06/views/styles.scss (excerpt)*

```
#like {
  p {
    font-weight: bold;
    color: $red;
  }
  input {
    background: $red url(/images/like.png) 0 2px no-repeat;
    border: darken($red, 10%) 1px solid;
    height: 28px;
    padding-left: 24px;
  }
}
```

Save everything, start up the server, and you should be able to test out the "like" functionality. Have a go at "liking" some of the songs, as in Figure 6.3.

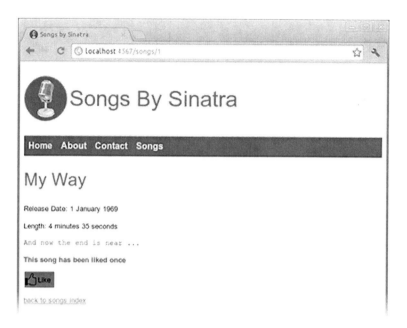

Figure 6.3. Testing the **Like** function

## Ajax

Reloading a whole page when only a small part of it has been updated is inefficient. This is because the whole page is returned from the server and reloaded, resulting in a poor user experience waiting for the page to refresh. Ajax can help us overcome this problem by loading content asynchronously in the background, so a page reload is unnecessary.

 **From Pop Sensation to Long Player**

Ajax used to be a buzzword in web development; now it's just one of the standard tools that people use when building web applications. The phrase was first coined by Jesse James Garrett in 2005 to stand for Asynchronous JavaScript And XML. It really took off, especially since Google were making extensive use of similar techniques in its Gmail and Google Maps applications with impressive results.

The term Ajax has stuck, however, and it's now a standard technique used by web applications to create interactions that take place without page reloads. The advent of frameworks such as jQuery has made it easy to implement and helped to iron out any browser inconsistencies. Using Ajax can make a web application feel a lot more responsive and more like a traditional desktop application.

## "Ajaxifying" the Like Button

Our **Like** button is a perfect candidate for using Ajax. A press of the button will update the number of "likes" a song has without the tedium of reloading the whole page. That the code for our **Like** button already works before Ajax is added is good, since it means it will work for browsers without JavaScript enabled, or which don't support `XMLHttpRequest` (this approach is known as progressive enhancement).

Adding Ajax functionality to our **Like** button is basically a three-step process:

1. Stop the actual request from happening when the button is pressed, so that we prevent the page from reloading.

2. Increase the number of "likes" by one and save it to the database behind the scenes.

3. Update the number of "likes" shown on the page, possibly with an effect to show this has happened.

To implement Ajax in our application, we update the code in **application.coffee** to include the following:

```
                                    chapter06/views/application.coffee (excerpt)

$ ->
  $('#released_on')
  .datepicker( changeYear: true, yearRange: '1940:2000' )
  $('#like input').click (event) -> ❶
    event.preventDefault() ❷
    $.post( ❸
      $('#like form').attr('action') ❹
      (data) -> $('#like p').html(data)
      .effect('highlight', color: '#fcd') ❺
    )
```

❶ This line searches for the `input` button inside the `div` with an `id` of `like` using CSS-style syntax (`#like input`). We then attach an event listener that checks for when this button is clicked.

❷ When this happens, the default behavior is prevented using the `event.preventDefault()` function, so the form will *not* be posted.

**❸**  Instead, an Ajax POST request is sent using the `$.post` function.

**❹**  This is sent to the URL contained in the form's `action` attribute, which we can access using `$('#like form').attr('action')`.

**❺**  The last line ensures the data that's returned will then be placed inside the paragraph element that is inside the "like" `div` (`#like p` in CSS selector syntax). We also add a little highlight flash as a visual cue for the user to show that the paragraph has been updated using the `effect` function, `effect('highlight', color: '#fcd')`.

At the moment, no data is returned by the server; we need to modify the route handler to act differently if Ajax is used. Sinatra has a neat helper method for this called `request.xhr?` that returns `true` if the request was made using Ajax and `false` if not. Open up **song.rb** and update the `like` route handler to be as follows:

chapter06/song.rb *(excerpt)*

```
post '/songs/:id/like' do
  @song = find_song
  @song.likes = @song.likes.next
  @song.save
  redirect to"/songs/#{@song.id}" unless request.xhr?
  slim :like, :layout => false
end
```

With this change, we only redirect back to the same page if the request was initiated by the user via Ajax. If the redirect fails, we return the HTML produced from the **like.slim** partial. This snippet of HTML is inserted into the web page using JavaScript. We need to set the `layout` to `false`, otherwise the layout will also be returned and repeated on the page.

## Pushing the Changes Live

Now that we have added a bit of pizzazz using JavaScript, it's time to push these changes to our live server and show the world. Before we do this, we'll merge our **Like** button functionality back into the master branch. It's a work pattern that's worth becoming used to as you experiment with new features in an application. To start with, we need to add and commit the changes to the like branch:

```
$ git add .
$ git commit -m 'Added a Like button'
```

Next, we change back to the master branch and merge the changes from the like branch:

```
$ git checkout master
$ git merge like
```

Now the master branch has the **Like** button functionality, so we can safely remove the like branch using the `-d` flag:

```
$ git branch -d like
```

We are almost ready to push these changes to Heroku, but since we've used some new gems, we need to add the following lines to the Gemfile:

chapter06/Gemfile *(excerpt)*

```
gem "coffee-script"
gem "therubyracer"
```

We then use Bundler to install these new gems:

```
$ bundle install
```

Now we are ready to push the changes to Heroku, using what should now be the familiar three commands:

```
$ git add .
$ git commit -m 'installed coffeescipt and rubyracer gems using bun
↪dler'
$ git push heroku master
```

This should deploy all our changes to the live site. One last task is to make sure the database on Heroku is updated. To do this, we log in to a console session on Heroku and then utilize the same commands we used locally earlier:

```
$ heroku run console
Running `console` attached to terminal... up, run.1
irb> require './main'
=> true
irb> DataMapper.auto_upgrade!
```

## All That Jazz

We've really applied some gloss on our application in this chapter. We've used CoffeeScript to create JavaScript and employed the jQuery and jQuery UI libraries to improve the user experience with a calendar widget.

We've also added a **Like** button to each song page enabling users to "like" a song. Ajax gives this a snappy feel, but it also works fine without JavaScript present.

Before you move on to the next and final chapter, have a look at the jQuery and jQuery UI websites to see what other bits of functionality could be added to your application. I'm sure you'll find lots of cool features that would further enhance it.

In the final chapter, we'll look at using Sinatra's modular architecture to help make the application easier to maintain and reuse in future.

Chapter **7**

# The Final Act

We've finished building our application now; it does everything it needs to do, so no more functionality will be added. This chapter is all about making our app more maintainable by switching to a modular structure. We'll look at how to create a modular-style application in Sinatra and discuss the benefits of doing so. I will demonstrate this by separating the website and song files into separate modules, and use Rack to route the URLs to the correct module.

We'll cover how easy it is to use Sinatra to create Rack middleware applications that can be used in other Sinatra applications, as well as other Rack-based frameworks such as Ruby on Rails. To demonstrate this, we'll create our own asset handler middleware to help make using CoffeeScript and CSS preprocessors easier in our application, as well as in future projects.

Then we will finish off by looking at the Padrino framework, which is based on Sinatra's modular structure.

# Modular Sinatra Applications

So far, all the applications we've seen in this book have been in the classic style. These use the top-level DSL of Ruby, meaning that all the methods exist in the top-level scope of the `main` object. The application itself is represented by the Sinatra::Application object.

It is also possible to build **modular applications** that use separate classes. Using separate classes means that the global namespace is not polluted, as all the methods will be defined in the scope of a specific class.[1] Using the modular style also allows multiple Sinatra applications for each Ruby process.

 **Modular versus Classic**

> Modular-style applications are more suited to complex applications and those that are created by multiple developers. It's fine to use the classic style in most use cases—often it's the most suitable and immediate way of doing things!

Here's a basic example of a modular application:

```
require 'sinatra/base'

class ModularApp < Sinatra::Base
  set :name, "Modular App"
  get '/' do
    "Hello from #{settings.name}"
  end

  run! if __FILE__ == $0
end
```

The route handlers (and configuration, helpers, and settings) are all placed inside a class that inherits from Sinatra::Base. It's important that we require `'sinatra/base'` rather than `'sinatra'`, as this would trigger creating a classic-style application.

---

[1] This usually isn't a problem for most applications, but if you planned to release your application as a gem it could be; any methods with the same name in other gems would cause conflicts, although Sinatra does take a number of steps to try to stop this becoming an issue.

Another difference with modular-style applications is that we have to explicitly start the application using the `run!` method at the end of the class. The `if` condition at the end checks to see if the file was directly executed, rather than being used in a test or by a rackup file.

### When All Files Are Created Equal

`__FILE__` is a relative path to the current file in use and `$0` represents the name of the file that was executed from the command line. So checking that these two are equal will check if the file that required this one is the file that was executed, rather than, for example, a test file.

Routes and settings can also be defined outside of the class body like so:

```
ModularApp.get '/hello' do
  "Hello again"
end

ModularApp.set :name, "Mod App"
```

# Developing Modular Applications

The modular-style application can make it easier to develop large applications, particularly when working in teams. The application can be broken down into smaller modules for each feature and developed in a self-contained environment, possibly by different people. Each module would have its own route handlers and views that are developed independently, before being put together and served up by the main application.

## Modularizing Songs By Sinatra

We could make the Songs By Sinatra website modular by splitting the main website and song section into separate classes that could be developed independently of each other.

To do this, we'll be placing the code in **main.rb** in its own class. This file is mainly concerned with the website portion of our application, so we'll name the class `Website`. After all the requires in **main.rb**, let's open up our `Website` class, like so:

```
                                            chapter07/main.rb (excerpt)
require 'sinatra/base'
require 'slim'
require 'sass'
require 'sinatra/flash'
require 'pony'
require './sinatra/auth'
require 'v8'
require 'coffee-script'

class Website < Sinatra::Base
```

All modular applications need to be subclasses of Sinatra::Base in order to inherit all of Sinatra's methods, but without becoming a top-level DSL (which is what would happen if it inherited from Sinatra solely). After opening the Website class, we explicitly register any extensions we're using:

```
                                            chapter07/main.rb (excerpt)
class Website < Sinatra::Base
  register Sinatra::Auth
  register Sinatra::Flash
```

 **Registering Extensions**

Another big difference between modular applications is that extensions need to be explicitly registered. The Auth extension that we created in Chapter 5 has the following line at the bottom of the module:

```
register Auth
```

This automatically registers the extension in a classic-style application so that its routes and helper methods can be used. When using a modular-style application, we must register the extensions we wish to use explicitly in each class on a case-by-case basis. This gives us more granular control over which extensions are registered with which modules.

After this, we add the configuration and settings:

```ruby
register Sinatra::Flash

configure do
  enable :sessions
  set :username, 'frank'
  set :password, 'sinatra'
end

configure :development do
  set :email_address => 'smtp.gmail.com',
    :email_user_name => 'daz',
    :email_password => 'secret',
    :email_domain => 'localhost.localdomain'
end

configure :production do
  set :email_address => 'smtp.sendgrid.net',
    :email_user_name => ENV['SENDGRID_USERNAME'],
    :email_password => ENV['SENDGRID_PASSWORD'],
    :email_domain => 'heroku.com'
end
```

These are just like before, although the configuration for the databases has been removed and will later be placed in the `SongController` class, as the database is only used by songs.

The `before` filter comes next, and stays the same as it was before:

```ruby
before do
  set_title
end
```

Next, we'll define the helper methods. The helper block is no longer necessary as helper methods are actually just class methods, so they become plain old methods of the `Website` class:

```ruby
def css(*stylesheets)
  ⋮
end

def current?(path='/')
  (request.path==path || request.path==path+'/') ? "current" : nil
end

def set_title
  @title ||= "Songs By Sinatra"
end

def send_message
  ⋮
end
```

After this, the routes stay the same as before:

```ruby
def send_message
  ⋮
end

get('/styles.css'){ scss :styles }
get('/javascripts/application.js'){ coffee :application }

get '/' do
  slim :home
end

get '/about' do
  ⋮
end

get '/contact' do
  slim :contact
end

not_found do
  slim :not_found
end
```

```
post '/contact' do
  ⋮
end
```

And last of all, remember to close the new `Website` class at the end of the file:

```
  post '/contact' do
    ⋮
  end
end
```

# Song Controller Module

In the **song.rb** file, we'll create a `SongController` class that is also a subclass of `Sinatra::Base`. This is where we place all the settings, helpers, and route handlers for songs, keeping them separate from the actual `Song` class that contains all the business logic for songs.

First of all, we must update our require statements:

```
require 'sinatra/base'
require 'dm-core'
require 'dm-migrations'
require 'slim'
require 'sass'
require 'sinatra/flash'
require './sinatra/auth'
```

Then the following code goes after the `SongHelpers` module in **song.rb**. Here, we register the extensions that this class will use, as well as any helper modules:

```
module SongHelpers
  ⋮
end

class SongController < Sinatra::Base
```

```
  enable :method_override
  register Sinatra::Flash
  register Sinatra::Auth

  helpers SongHelpers
```

Way back in the section called "Editing Songs" in Chapter 3, we used some hidden
form fields with the name of _method so that we could use PUT and DELETE HTTP
methods, even though they lack browser support. This is known as method overrid-
ing; the method_override setting is enabled by default in classic applications, but
not in modular applications. This means that we'll have to explicitly enable it in
the Song class in order for the update and delete routes to behave as expected and
map to the correct route handlers.

After this, we'll take the database configuration settings that we removed from the
Website class and place them inside the SongController class:

*chapter07/song.rb (excerpt)*

```
helpers SongHelpers

configure do
  enable :sessions
  set :username, 'frank'
  set :password, 'sinatra'
end

configure :development do
  DataMapper.setup(:default, "sqlite3://#{Dir.pwd}/development.db")
end

configure :production do
  DataMapper.setup(:default, ENV['DATABASE_URL'])
end
```

After the configuration settings, we add some of the helper methods that we used
in the Website class, as well as the before filter. This is because they are utilized
in the layout that's employed by both the Website and SongController classes:

```
configure :production do
  DataMapper.setup(:default, ENV['DATABASE_URL'])
end

before do
  set_title
end

def css(*stylesheets)
  stylesheets.map do |stylesheet|
    "<link href=\"/#{stylesheet}.css\" media=\"screen, projection\"
⇒rel=\"stylesheet\" />"
  end.join
end

def current?(path='/')
  (request.path==path || request.path==path+'/') ? "current" : nil
end

def set_title
  @title ||= "Songs By Sinatra"
end
```

*chapter07/song.rb (excerpt)*

Last of all come the route handlers, but the big change here is that the routes are no longer prefixed with /songs. Instead, this will be added to the URL by the Rack router. It needs to be set up in the **config.ru** file, and is covered in the section called "Rack Routing":

*chapter07/song.rb (excerpt)*

```
get '/' do
  find_songs
  slim :songs
end

get '/new' do
  protected!
  @song = Song.new
  slim :new_song
end

get '/:id' do
```

```
    @song = find_song
    slim :show_song
  end

  get '/:id/edit' do
    protected!
    @song = find_song
    slim :edit_song
  end

  post '/' do
    protected!
    create_song
    if create_song
      flash[:notice] = "Song successfully added"
    end
    redirect to("/#{@song.id}")
  end

  put '/:id' do
    protected!
    song = find_song
    if song.update(params[:song])
      flash[:notice] = "Song successfully updated"
    end
    redirect to("/#{song.id}")
  end

  delete '/:id' do
    protected!
    if find_song.destroy
      flash[:notice] = "Song deleted"
    end
    redirect to('/')
  end

  post '/:id/like' do
    @song = find_song
    @song.likes = @song.likes.next
    @song.save
    redirect to("/#{@song.id}") unless request.xhr?
    slim :like, :layout => false
  end
end
```

# Rack Routing

Now that we've moved our application routes into a modular structure, we're able to utilize Rack to route our URLs based on some namespacing. This is done using the **config.ru** file. When the file is executed using run, we employ Rack to start the applications based on the URL entered (rather than running the application explicitly). Here's the code that should go in **config.ru**:

chapter07/config.ru

```
require 'sinatra/base'

require './main'
require './song'

map('/songs') { run SongController }
map('/') { run Website }
```

The map method is used to create a songs namespace for the Song class. This means that any URLs starting with /songs will be mapped to the route handlers in the SongController class.

 **Namespace Help**

Sinatra has a url helper method that can be used in views to add the correct namespace. So if the following link was produced in a view in the SongController, it would be mapped to /songs/about, rather than just /about:

```
a href=url('/about')
```

The to helper method that we've been using in our route handlers is just an alias for the url helper method, so it performs the same task.

Test it out by running **rackup** from the command prompt; by default, your Sinatra app should now be running on port 9292, so check out http://localhost:9292 and make sure it all works.

# Subclassing Modules

Once you've created some classes in the modular style, you can create subclasses of these. The subclass will inherit all the routes and settings from the parent class, but, as with Ruby methods in subclasses, any routes and settings defined in the subclass will override those in the parent class. Here's an example to demonstrate:

```ruby
require 'sinatra/base'

class App < Sinatra::Base
  set :name, "App"

  get '/' do
    "this is the app"
  end

  get '/hello' do
    "Hello, this is #{settings.name}"
  end
end

class Sub < App
  set :name, "Sub"

  get '/' do
    "This is the sub app"
  end
end

Sub.run!
```

To try this out, save this code in a file called **subclass.rb**; then, open up a terminal and navigate to where the file is saved and type `ruby subclass.rb`.

In this example, the `Sub` class inherits the routes and settings in the `App` class, but we then override the / route handler and `:name` setting. So if you visit http://localhost:4567/, the message `This is the sub app` is displayed, and if you visit http://localhost:4567/hello, you'll see the message, `Hello, this is Sub`.

### Create a Parent Class to Keep It DRY

You might have found it annoying (and not at all DRY) that we had to register many of the same extensions and define many of the helper methods in both the `Website` and `Song` class. The solution is to create a parent class (called, for example, `ApplicationController`), that registers all extensions and helper methods. The `Website` and `SongController` classes can then inherit from this class. The code would look like this:

```
class ApplicationController < Sinatra::Base
  register Sinatra::Flash
  register Sinatra::Auth
end

class Website < ApplicationController
  ⋮
end

class Song < ApplicationController
  ⋮
end
```

# Middleware

Remember Figure 1.1 from way back in Chapter 1? Figure 7.1 shows the traditional client-server model.

Figure 7.1. The traditional client-server model returns for an encore

Middleware is a layer of software sitting between the client and server that offers extra functionality. You can have any number of middleware stacked in between the server and the client, as shown in Figure 7.2.

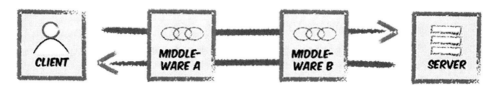

Figure 7.2. Middleware sitting pretty in the middle

In the Ruby world, Rack is used to manage middleware by organizing all the different middleware applications into a stack and then serving them in order.

Because all the major Ruby frameworks operate with Rack, middleware can be written in Sinatra and then applied, for example, in a Rails application using Rails Metal. In fact, there are a large number of Ruby gems that act as middleware, providing all sorts of functionality such as authentication, caching, and stopping spam prevention.

## Asset Middleware

We have been using SCSS to create CSS since the section called "Getting Sassy" in Chapter 2 and CoffeeScript for JavaScript since Chapter 6. This required us to add the following route handlers:

```
get('/styles.css'){ scss :styles }
get('/javascripts/application.js'){ coffee :application }
```

Let's have a go at moving this functionality into middleware that will allow our application to use CoffeeScript to produce JavaScript, and provide a choice of CSS preprocessors for CSS. It makes sense to move this functionality to middleware, as it can then be reused in future applications. To start with, remove the two route handlers from the Website class in **main.rb** and create a new file called **asset-handler.rb** containing the following code:

chapter07/asset-handler.rb *(excerpt)*

```
class AssetHandler < Sinatra::Base
```

First of all, we make our AssetHandler class a subclass of Sinatra::Base, which is the same for all Sinatra middleware. After this, we'll include some default settings in a configure block that will make our middleware more flexible for future use:

chapter07/asset-handler.rb *(excerpt)*

```ruby
class AssetHandler < Sinatra::Base
  configure do
    set :views, File.dirname(__FILE__) + '/assets'
    set :jsdir, 'js'
    set :cssdir, 'css'
    enable :coffeescript
    set :cssengine, 'scss'
  end
```

The :views setting is used to change the views folder to one called **assets**. This is where we'll keep all our asset files. We also have settings for the folder names where the CoffeeScript and SCSS files are kept within the **assets** directory; the default setting is a subdirectory called js for the CoffeeScript files, and a subdirectory called css for the SCSS files.

The :coffeescript setting is enabled by default, but can be disabled if we don't want to use CoffeeScript to compile JavaScript. If this is set to false, the routes will simply point to a JavaScript file in the public directory.

Last of all, the :cssengine setting allows us to choose which CSS preprocessor to use. We'll set the default to scss as this is what we've been using throughout the book, but it could be changed to less or sass if desired.

Now we'll add two route handlers that catch all routes ending in .js and .css:

chapter07/asset-handler.rb *(excerpt)*

```ruby
    set :cssengine, 'scss'
  end

  get '/javascripts/*.js' do ❶
    pass unless settings.coffeescript? ❷
    coffee (settings.jsdir + '/' + params[:splat].first).to_sym ❸
  end

  get '/*.css' do
    send(settings.cssengine, (settings.cssdir + '/' + params[:splat]
➥.first).to_sym) ❹
  end
end ❺
```

**1** The first route handler picks up any links to JavaScript files. Since it is impossible to know in advance what the names of the JavaScript and CSS files might be, we use the wildcard "*" symbol in the routes.

**2** The `pass` method is used to simply pass over this handler and find another matching route if the `:coffeescript` setting is `false`. If it is `true`, however, the `coffee` method is used to display the file with the same name as the JavaScript file requested in the directory specified by the `:jsdir` directory.

**3** Given that we're using a wildcard in the route handler, any route used will be contained in the `params[:splat]` array. Therefore, any number of JavaScript links can be added without us requiring any new route handlers; the middleware will pick these routes up and deal with them accordingly.

**4** The second route handler uses the `send` method; since it's impossible to know in advance which preprocessor to use, we don't know which method to use. The `send` method lets us invoke a method from the string stored in the `:cssengine` setting.

**5** Before we finish, we make sure to close the class.

### Misplaced Files

Remember to move the **application.coffee** file into an **/assets/js** folder and the **styles.scss** file into an **/assets/css** folder.

## Using Middleware

To use our new `AssetHandler` middleware, we require the **asset-handler.rb** file and add the `use` method in any classes that use it. We only need it in the `Website` class, so add the following to **main.rb**:

```
                                                    chapter07/main.rb (excerpt)

require './asset-handler'

class Website < Sinatra::Base
  use AssetHandler
```

**Relative Requires**

The line `require './asset-handler'` looks a bit messy, with the period and slash at the front. If you want to tidy up your require statements, there are two ways of doing it.

If you're running Ruby 1.9 or higher, you could use the `require_relative` method. This requires files relative to where the current file is located, so instead of the `require` statement we just used, we could simply write:

```
require_relative 'asset-handler'
```

The other option is to add the current directory to Ruby's load path. The **load path** is an array of all the places where Ruby should look for files that have been required (the directory where gems are stored is already in the load path, which is why there's no need to specify where these are when you require them). Using the following line of code before your `require` statements will add the current directory to the load path:

```
$: << '.'
```

Now you can require the files as normal (that is, without the `./`):

```
require 'asset-handler'
```

If you're running a version of Ruby lower than 1.9 (though you really shouldn't be!), the current directory is already in the load path, so you can just require the files like this anyway.

## Caching

We can improve the performance of our asset handler by adding support for caching. This is done by setting HTTP headers so that the page is only requested if it's been updated with the `last_modified` header (a date) and the `etag` header. An **ETag**, or entity tag, is a string used to identify the version of a resource such as a web page. If a resource changes, its `etag` should change to reflect this.

Sinatra has some useful helper methods for controlling caching, such as `expires`, `cache_control`, `last_modified`, and `etag`. These can be used to set the HTTP headers so that Sinatra will check whether a page has been modified before requesting it from the server. If no modification has been made, the page will use a cached version and return a HTTP status code of 304 instead of 200.

We're going to set the `last_modified` headers for our assets according to the last time the directories were modified using the `mtime` method of the `File` object. For example, the following line of code can be used to set the `last_modified` header for the JavaScript assets:

```
last_modified File.mtime(settings.root+'/assets/'+settings.jsdir)
```

To add caching for our assets, change the route handler code in **asset-handler.rb** to the following:

*chapter07/asset-handler.rb (excerpt)*

```
get '/javascripts/*.js' do
  pass unless settings.coffeescript?
  last_modified File.mtime(settings.root+'/assets/'+settings.jsdir)
  cache_control :public, :must_revalidate
  coffee (settings.jsdir + '/' + params[:splat].first).to_sym
end

get '/*.css' do
  last_modified File.mtime(settings.root+'/assets/'+settings.cssdir)
  cache_control :public, :must_revalidate
  send(settings.cssengine, (settings.cssdir + '/' + params[:splat]
➥.first).to_sym)
end
```

 ### Cache Controls

The `:public` setting means that any intermediary cache (such as an ISP's proxy server) can also cache the content in addition to the client. If the data is of a sensitive nature, you could use the `:private` setting, which only allows cached content to be stored on the local client.

The `:must_revalidate` setting indicates that the client or intermediary cache must confirm that the content is still up to date on every request.

If you start the application running and then check the server logs in the terminal window, you should see status codes of 304 for the **/javascripts/application.js** and **/styles.css** (assuming you've left the files untouched!).

 ## Set Your Headers Globally to Save on Server Load Time

A neat trick for setting the `last_modified` and `etag` headers globally is to use the application's start time. While this may not strictly be the actual time all files were last modified, we can usually assume that if the application has been restarted, something has been changed; therefore, it's worth flushing the cache out and reloading the pages anyway.

To do this, the following setting needs to be placed inside a configure block:

```
configure do
  set :start_time, Time.now
end
```

Because the code inside a configure block is only run once when an application starts, this setting will effectively provide the start time of the application. We can then use this for the `last_modified` header and convert it to a string for the `etag` header.

It can then be used to apply caching to all the pages in our website using this `before` filter:

```
before do
  last_modified settings.start_time
  etag settings.start_time.to_s
  cache_control :public, :must_revalidate
end
```

This is a useful way of reducing the load on the server in an application by avoiding any needless round trips to the server.

Now is a good time to push your updates to Heroku.

## Middleware Settings

The settings in the asset handler middleware could be changed by editing the **asset-handler.rb** file directly. This isn't ideal, as we'd prefer to just leave this file as it is, particularly if it's to be used in other projects. Thankfully, it is possible to change the settings from within the `Website` class (or anywhere else in our application). This is because settings are actually just methods of the `AssetHandler` class, so we can simply override those methods to change them. For example, if we didn't want to use CoffeeScript, we could disable it using the following line:

```
AssetHandler.disable :coffeescript
```

### Better Assets

This is a basic example of an asset handler. If you want a more robust and feature-rich option, there are a number to consider such as:

- Rake::Pipeline https://github.com/livingsocial/rake-pipeline
- Sinatra AssetPack https://github.com/rstacruz/sinatra-assetpack
- Sprockets https://github.com/sstephenson/sprockets

# Rolling Your Own Framework

Using the modular style, along with extensions and middleware, Sinatra becomes extremely flexible. It does not force you to use any particular type of architecture, so there's nothing stopping you from creating your own bespoke microframework that fits your needs perfectly. You can choose which database ORM, folder layout, and rendering engine to use. Additional functionality is possible with Sinatra extensions and Rack middleware.

For example, we could create a Rails-like MVC structure. In Figure 7.3, I'm including a `Song` model to demonstrate how our Songs By Sinatra site might look using this framework.

Figure 7.3. Rolling our own Rails structure in Sinatra

The controllers would contain all the route handlers. In the **controller** directory, we could create an `ApplicationController` class that is a subclass of `Sinatra::Base`. This would set up all the views and layouts used by the whole application, and also register any application-wide extensions:

```
class ApplicationController < Sinatra::Base
end
```

Other controllers, such as the `WebsiteController` and `SongController`, would then inherit from this class:

```
WebsiteController < ApplicationController
end
SongController < ApplicationController
end
```

**application_helper.rb** would contain all the helpers used by the overall application. Other helper files, such as **website_helper** and **song_helper.rb**, could be used for model-specific helper methods.

The **config.ru** file could then be used to require all the relevant files and serve the controllers based on the URLs provided:

```
require 'sinatra/base'
Dir.glob('./{helpers,controllers}/*.rb').each {|file| require file }

map('/songs') { run SongController }
map('/') { run WebsiteController }
```

As an exercise, try refactoring the Songs By Sinatra application to fit this framework structure. You could then develop a custom framework solution that works for you.

# Padrino

Creating your own framework is great fun and gives you an unprecedented level of control, but sometimes you just want to start building an application with some of the setup and configuration already done for you. If this is the case, I'd recommend checking out Padrino,[2] a framework based on Sinatra.

Padrino leverages the modular structure amazingly well to create a robust full-stack framework with all the features, and it still manages to be lightweight in comparison to other frameworks such as Ruby on Rails. It is also agnostic to which database ORM, testing framework, and JavaScript library is chosen.

Padrino includes a number of built-in components such as an administration interface, caching support, code generators, view helpers, internationalization support, and email controls. All of these components are optional, so you can add and remove them as your application needs them.

---

[2] http://www.padrinorb.com/

They can also be added as standalone components to Sinatra applications. This is useful if your application requires only some of the functionality without the extra overhead of the full framework. Padrino is a great example of building on top of Sinatra's foundation, so I would definitely recommend looking at the source code on GitHub.[3]

# In a Class of Its Own

We made no changes to how the application functions in this chapter. Instead, we broke it down into separate modules that could be developed independently of each other, making it more flexible and easier to maintain. We also used Rack to route each module to a namespaced URL.

After this, we looked at how middleware fits into the Rack ecosystem and how Sinatra can be used to build middleware. We built a simple asset handler middleware that helps to serve CoffeeScript and SCSS files in our Sinatra application, as well as being easily configurable for use in other applications.

Finally, we investigated the possibility of using Sinatra to build your own framework for developing web applications. We finished off by looking at the Padrino framework, which is a great example of a modular Sinatra application.

# Start Spreading the News ...

I hope that through reading this book, you have learned enough about Sinatra to go forward and start building your own exciting websites, web applications, and web services.

We have covered a lot in a short space, culminating in a modular, database-driven site. You should now have all the tools you need to press on and start building your own web tools using Sinatra and huge dollops of your own imagination. The only thing holding you back is your own technical ability and inventiveness. Sinatra is inherently flexible and lets you work in any way you wish.

Now that you've finished this book, your journey with Sinatra is just beginning. Read online posts, participate in forums, and ask questions. Most of all, experiment! There are no barriers when it comes to building an application with Sinatra, so try

---

[3] https://github.com/padrino/padrino-framework

as many approaches as you can and keep developing your skills. You can use Sinatra to build a small website, test out some code quickly, build a web interface for an existing Ruby program, or build a fully fledged modular web application. There are endless possibilities.

Have fun!

# Index

username, changing, 104

**V**

V8 JavaScript engine, 106
variables
   CSS preprocessor variables, 34
   ERB and variable assignments, 16–17
   instance variables, 28–30
   named parameters and, 8–10
   settings, 68
verbs (*see* HTTP verbs)
views
   (*see also* layouts)
   dynamic views, 16–17
   ERB and, 15–16
   external, 20–22
   partials, 33–34
views folder, 21

**W**

website construction
   (*see also* forms)
   architecture choice in Sinatra, 140–142
   basic, 13–38
   connecting Ruby to the web, 49
   CRUD operations, 45–49
   deploying the website, 75–81
   developing modular applications, 123–130
   example (Songs By Sinatra), 13–14
   making changes live, 118–119
   page uploading, 116
   record collection, 39–63
   with CoffeeScript, 105–120
Windows installations, 4, 40

**Z**

zero versus nil, 113

# Congratulations on Finishing the Book

## See yourself as Sinatra-savvy?

Time to test yourself with our online quiz. With questions based on the content in the book, only the sharpest Sinatra virtuosos can achieve a perfect score.

## Take the Quiz Here:

http://quizpoint.com/#categories/SINATRA

# Hey ...

## Thanks for buying this book. We really appreciate your support!

We'd like to think that you're now a "Friend of SitePoint," and so would like to invite you to our special "Friends of SitePoint" page.

Here you can SAVE up to 43% on a range of other super-cool SitePoint products.

### Save over 40% with this link:

Link: 🌐 sitepoint.com/friends

Password: friends